WHY DO PEOPLE LOVE AMERICA?

Printed and bound in Great Britain by MPG Books Ltd, Bodmin

Distributed in the US by Publishers Group West

Arcane is an imprint of Sanctuary Publishing Limited
Sanctuary House, 45–53 Sinclair Road
London W14 0NS, United Kingdom

www.sanctuarypublishing.com

Cover design: Ash

ISBN: 1-86074-614-4

WHY DO PEOPLE LOVE AMERICA?

LOUIS CHUNOVIC

Sanctuary

For my parents, Charlotte and Abraham

Contents

'We're simultaneously the most loved, feared, admired and hated nation in the world. In short, we're Frank Sinatra.'

– Dennis Miller, actor/comedian/commentator, to a gathering of television critics, January 2004

About The Author

Louis Chunovic is a print and broadcast journalist and the author of more than a dozen books, both novels and non-fiction. He is the former Television Editor of *The Hollywood Reporter* newspaper, the former Managing Editor of *Variety's On Production* magazine and the former on-air Entertainment Reporter for Fox Television in Los Angeles.

He has been interviewed and quoted by *The New York Times*, National Public Radio and *Congressional Quarterly Researcher*, among others, and has appeared on many national and local television and radio shows.

His books include *One Foot On The Floor: The Curious Evolution Of Sex On Television*, *Bruce Lee: The Tao Of The Dragon Warrior*, *The Rocky And Bullwinkle Book*, *Jodie: A Biography*, *Northern Exposure: The Book* and *Quantum Leap: The Book*.

He also is the author of *Marilyn Monroe At Twentieth Century Fox* (writing as Lawrence Crown), and the novels *Hyde And Seek* and *Hyde In Deep Cover* (writing as Benjamin Wolff).

Louis is also the author and editor of a privately printed history of the Hollywood Radio and Television Society, commissioned on the occasion of that organisation's 50th anniversary.

Other publications for which Louis has written include *Advertising Age*, *The Advocate*, *American Film*, *Boston Metro*, *Broadcasting & Cable*, *The California Apparel News*, *Electronic Media*, *Entertainment Weekly*, *The Fort Lauderdale Sun-Sentinel*, *The Journal Of The Writers Guild Of America*, *The Las Vegas Sun*, *The Los Angeles Business Journal*, *The*

Los Angeles Times, MovieLine, PC World, The Saint Paul Pioneer Press, The San Francisco Examiner, Screen Magazine, The Torrance Daily Breeze, TV Guide, US, Weekly Variety and many others.

Louis has recently completed a Hollywood novel and is working on a book about politics and the media.

Acknowledgements

My thanks to the good people of Sanctuary Publishing in London, and in particular to Albert DePetrillo, Senior Editor, who thought of me for this project, and to Chris Harvey, Project Editor, who made it his mission to see the manuscript safely through the production process. My thanks also to Claire Musters, a skilled and sensitive copy editor.

To Doc Feiler: a special thanks for the customary consultations.

Introduction
Greetings From The Capital Of The World

On that bright, beautiful September morning when terrorists flew airliners into the World Trade Center, I stood, aghast, on the far bank of the mighty Hudson River that borders Manhattan's West Side, watching the towers – the very incarnation of American industry and the American Dream – wreathed in smoke and flame. The world rallied to America the day the towers fell, and for a few brief months it seemed as if there was no Them and Us, just the bad guys and all the rest of us.

It didn't last of course.

I thought of my parents that day. This book is for them and this is why: my parents were survivors of the Nazi concentration camps, and America saved them.

America has saved millions, and not just once, not just Christians and not just Europeans.

That is not to say that everything in America is and always has been perfect, or that it's the best of all possible countries, or even that it's always done its very best in this troubled world.

But ask yourself this: Which country has saved more lives? Which country has figured more in people's most hopeful dreams?

I was born in Europe, in Prague to be precise. We moved to the United States when I was five, and I learned English on the streets of Manhattan's Lower East Side. So, from the very start, I appreciated what the USA had to offer, not only the colourful art of the comic books and the neon marquees of the cinemas glowing on every street corner, but sanctuary – and opportunity – for the likes of me, a street urchin from Mittel Europa.

But I'm not a love-it-or-leave-it booster. I grew up despising the old men in Washington who so carelessly sent young men to their deaths in foreign wars and foreign-policy misadventures. I still do. And this is not a gloom-and-doom book. *Au contraire*, boys and girls.

This is a book about the bling-bling. This is a book about the possibilities. And about the clothes, the shows, the music, the movies, the hope and the hype. And this is a book about the dreamers and the schemers, the grand Just Maybe Me Too at the beating heart of the American Dream. As well as the Dead Presidents that make most of it possible.

The American Dream is about hard work paying off, true enough, but it's about more than just that. In the Land of Opportunity anyone can get lucky too. In America, don't you know, anyone can become a millionaire, even, say, a retired 58-year-old New York schoolteacher named Guadalupe, who one Saturday night put $3 in a slot machine in an Atlantic City, New Jersey casino and – KA-CHING! – won a jackpot of $2,421,291.76.

Yippee!

How did she do it? 'Divine inspiration', the former schoolteacher explained. 'I have a great devotion to Our Lady of Guadalupe [for whom she is named] and said a little prayer. Our Lady really looks after me.'

Yes, she does. And oh by the way, Guadalupe Lopez's daughter is an actress-singer you might have heard of. She goes by the name of J Lo.

Despite everything – despite war, recession and those damn odds stacked against you that everyone's always griping about – your actual chances of making your million in today's America aren't all that bad. Currently, one out of 125 citizens is a millionaire – counting money alone and, significantly, not including home equity – according to a recent Wall Street survey, which also found that in 2003 the USA produced more of these new 'high net worth individuals' than any other country on earth. How good are those odds? Ask the Irish bar maid who came to New York City two decades ago with her husband, a construction worker. She waited on tables, they saved up their money and this year they are opening their third authentic Irish pub in the wealthy, leafy suburbs.

American pop culture is commercial, yes, trying to convince you to buy something – jeans perhaps – because all the pretty people wearing them are having such delicious fun. But no one will throw you in jail if you don't get right into those Rogans or Diesels.

Here's something to consider: if the Soviet Union, the Evil Empire of Recent Yore, had in fact become an economic powerhouse to rival the United States, exporting its wares and its culture throughout the world, instead of crumbling into just a historical footnote, it still would not have been nearly so influential as America has become.

The commissars of the USSR had their Five Year Plans; capitalists, both real and would-be, of the USA have their American Dreams. And of what do these people dream? They dream of lightning, the kind that strikes and changes everything overnight. It could happen to anyone – J Lo's mum, an overweight Black kid with a pleasing singing voice, a geeky college kid with a better idea, an immigrant working two jobs, one of the long line of greenhorns and newcomers – who today are from places like Bangladesh, the Dominican Republic, India, Mexico, Nigeria, Thailand or maybe the Israeli-occupied West Bank.

This dream has been the idea that's motivated scores of millions of dreamers and strivers throughout American history, and this is still The Dream today: One person with luck and pluck and vision and hard work (and most likely a few bucks set aside) – some guy nobody's ever heard of named Schultz or

Kroc or Gates – can look at something as prosaic as a coffee shop or a hamburger stand or a new machine and – Eureka! – come up with a way to standardise it, manufacture it or market it worldwide. Cheaper, better, faster! And voila!...

McDonald's, Starbucks and Microsoft arise.

Is it easy? No. But is it possible?... Potentially no one in America with a good idea is out of that opportunity loop.

No one in America is unworthy, unclean or untouchable, simply by birth. No woman has to put on the burka, the veil or the hijab (the Muslim woman's traditional headscarf). Unless of course she wants to. And then no one can stop her. And if they try, there's recourse to the courts. After all, America is a land of laws. There are protections for individual citizens, including the famous Bill Of Rights. So in America who can deny even a poor Muslim girl her First Amendment right to wear the hijab?

The French may argue that this is not entirely to the good. In the United States, when an 11-year-old Muslim girl in Oklahoma was recently prohibited from wearing her headscarf in school, her parents sued and won. It was a matter of religious rights and personal expression, they argued, and the law agreed. In France, however, a recent and controversial law was passed that prohibits the headscarf in public schools, and there, that law has also been upheld.

France has the largest Muslim population of any European country. Nearly ten per cent of its citizens are Muslims, some five million in all, and mostly they originate from France's former North African colonies – the majority are of Algerian, Moroccan or Tunisian descent. Many of these French Muslims, who often suffer racism and are relegated to menial jobs when they are not enduring high rates of unemployment, live in high-rise projects in the Paris suburbs, built specifically to house them. The projects are in reality high-rise ghettos, where fundamentalism and a kind of tribal gang rule thrive, and where young Muslim women in particular have been oppressed by their co-religionists. The French argument for the law against the headscarf in school goes something like this: Muslim girls and women are second-class citizens in their own societies and their own families, and they are forced to wear the headscarf, which brands them as unequal. But the idea of equality demands that in the public sphere – or at least in the public school – they have some state sanction for equal treatment and equal opportunity. Of course, framed that way the argument sounds quite all-American.

But it is the act of *overcoming* that is really quintessentially American – turning your liability into an asset, making lemonade out of your lemon, taking that symbol of second-class status and making it over into a distinctive and valuable brand.

After all, isn't America all about the pursuit – of riches, of fame, of power and, of course, of pleasure – a pursuit that America democratised?

Of course, first you have to get here – and to many around the world, the history of America is all about this one very big idea: Anybody who can get over to America can, potentially, get over. Poland to polo in one generation, as the old Hollywood saying goes. That opportunity is even enshrined in the Cuban Adjustment Act, a most peculiar law drafted during the Clinton era and aimed specifically at the Cubans fleeing Castro in pursuit of The Dream, the ones who turn up regularly on the Miami nightly news, the ones who've dared to cross the choppy, treacherous Florida strait, risking sharks and sudden storms, in all manner of fanciful and fearful water craft, including strapped-together inner tubes and, believe it or not, an old, beat-up pick-up truck outfitted with an outboard motor and makeshift water wings. The law, which only applies to Cubans, is a recognition of the immense political clout this tightly knit immigrant group wields in its adopted Florida home. In essence, the law states that if the United States Coast Guard, patrolling the waters off the Florida shores, spots would-be refugees on the high seas, these 'wet foot' Cubans can be (and routinely are) plucked off their vessels and sent back to El Commandante's waiting arms.

But.

If they can just somehow swim and splash their way to shore – actually, physically, touch the golden American sand – the so-called 'dry foot' Cubans are allowed to stay. And so, to this day, small groups of waterlogged and bedraggled refugees are spotted regularly bobbing a few hundred yards off Miami's packed tourist beaches. Some are promptly snatched up by Coast Guard ships and helicopters and returned to Cuba while others, sometimes half-drowned after their long ordeal, are pulled onto land spontaneously by passing strangers on the beach, who know about the 'dry foot' law and want to bring the Cubans in. And that's their first welcome to their new homes.

(Haitians, of course, on the next Caribbean island over, also hunger for The Dream, and they try to flee their own island's miseries and corruptions, too. But unlike the Cubans, the illegal Haitian immigrants have no electoral clout, so they are all wet feet as far as the law is concerned. But that's another story…)

Uninfluential unfortunates without the Cuban Exemption aside, America still fosters the notion that somewhere inside everyone is the same spirit and pluck that once motivated the heroic age of exploration and empire-building.

Ask Mark Burnett, the Dagenham-born British subject who created *Survivor* – and his own American television empire – if America is not hospitable to individual merit and good ideas. Burnett is a 40-something child of the East End who enlisted in the British Army and served with the Parachute Regiment in Northern Ireland and the Falklands, then travelled to America on a whim. In the process of finding his destiny, this ex-paratrooper worked as – of all things – a Beverly Hills nanny and a T-shirt salesman on sun-soaked Venice Beach in Los Angeles, before coming up with the brainstorm that changed his life – and, eventually, American television. His idea was for a reality show about a rugged physical competition that takes brains as well as brawn to survive! *Survivor* went on to beget Burnett's *The Apprentice*, the surprise hit of the 2003–2004 American television season, with New York real estate mogul Donald Trump, he of the beady stare, the pursed lips and the indomitable comb over, pronouncing weekly to one would-be Master of the Universe after another, 'You're fired!'

In the final episode, when The Donald finally pronounced 'You're hired' for the first time, the winner of the $250,000 (£155,000) a year job with Trump's organisation, a youngish Internet entrepreneur from Chicago, offered this assessment of The Meaning of It All:

'The American Dream is still alive out there, and hard work will get you there! You don't necessarily need to have an Ivy League education or to have millions of dollars start-up money. It can be done with an idea, hard work and determination.'

Burnett's whole life, he has said repeatedly, is an example of the American Dream, and that's what his shows are about, too.

There used to be a rather smug rule of thumb in the Ficus-fronded, Chippendale-furnished executive suites of the upper echelons of the American television business: Americans were xenophobic when it came to the home box, went the conventional wisdom, and they simply would not watch anything on TV that was not homegrown. Mark Burnett has put an end to that idea, once and for all, but it was never truly true. After all, *All In The Family*, arguably the greatest success of American television comedy ever, the show that riveted the nation in the 1970s, was derived from a British 'format', namely, *Till Death Do Us Part*.

And more recently, the biggest hits of so-called reality TV have originated outside of North America, too. *American Idol* and *Who Wants To Be A Millionaire?* both derive from hits in the United Kingdom, *Big Brother* started out in the Netherlands and *Fear Factor* is an import from Australia.

America, ever on the lookout for Next Big Thing, for the new and the trendy, does tend to treat the rest of the world, and Europe in particular, as a laboratory of hip, cherry-picking the Euro-best in every field. America's media entrepreneurs have learned to take a concept from beyond America's shores and then re-sell it to American audiences as an original. That may smack of chutzpah, but it does work. And it works, too, when the same entrepreneurs take their non-American 'American' successes and sell them back again, ten times over, to the rest of the world.

The Beatles may have been famous Liverpudlians, 'moptops' playing American rhythm 'n' blues with a British accent in their hometown's dive bars, but it was only after they travelled to New York and appeared on *The Ed Sullivan Show*, to be viewed by the largest single TV audience to that date (73 million viewers, 60 per cent of the people watching the tube at that hour); only after they were touched by the magic of American television and American enthusiasm, that they were transformed into a worldwide cultural phenomenon.

The Beatles were quickly followed by what came to be known as the British Invasion of American popular music. Before long, the pop charts were dominated by the likes of not just the Fab Four, but The Rolling Stones, The Animals, The Kinks, The Dave Clark Five, Herman's Hermits, Chad And Jeremy, Gerry And The Pacemakers, Peter And Gordon, The Zombies and, of course, The Who, whose early 1966 US hit was 'My Generation'. This had Roger Daltrey exuberantly shouting out, 'Why don't you all f- fade away!' Everybody knew what he really meant, but nobody in America could put him in jail for it, although surely there were powerful American elders who fumed with righteous outrage and wished they could.

Ironic, then, that many of these same British bands, but particularly The Beatles and the Stones, first became popular in America playing vintage American rhythm 'n' blues, the music that Jagger, Richards, Lennon and McCartney first heard as kids in the 1950s – the songs of Howlin' Wolf, Elmore James, Muddy Waters and Chuck Berry, to name just a few.

In fact, Jagger and Richards began playing music together in 1960 only after Richards ran into Jagger on the London subway and discovered that the records Jagger was carrying, records that he'd just gotten in the mail from Chess Records, were by the very same Chicago blues artists that Richards had always loved.

All around the world people love the sounds of American music, whether it's rock, jazz or hip-hop, not for just the beat or the melody, but for all that it represents. But these days of course, the sounds of music have to contend with the clamour of war.

The critics claim that America fights its wars for United Fruit or for Halliburton or for Big Oil, just as they used to say that Britain fights for the interests of the East India Company. True enough, politicians and princes, whether hereditary or of commerce, tend to have their own parochial ideas about what's worth (mostly other people) fighting and dying for.

But the American people themselves do not fight for Big Oil. They fight only for the Big Idea.

And in America, the politicians and the princes must have a care to convince the people that there's a Big Idea; otherwise, they risk that the people will throw them out.

There was no oil in Kosovo when America and NATO bombed Belgrade in the late 1990s, just a civilian Muslim population that was in danger of being wiped out in the despicable practice of 'ethnic cleansing'.

Even now, after nearly 3,000 innocent civilians were killed by the Al Qaeda suicide-hijacker fanatics bent on restoring the Caliphate and the rule of Shariah (strict Islamic law), and on cleansing the Holy Lands of 'crusaders and Jews', Americans are not at war with Islam, no matter what people are told in the extremist religious schools, the madrassahs, and on the Arab street.

'Most of the Muslim people in the Mideast do not know that the last time we used military power it was to help Muslims in Bosnia and Kosovo. They do not know that America advocated, Israel accepted, but the [Palestine Liberation Organization] rejected, the most generous offer to establish a Palestinian state,' said former United States President Bill Clinton, whose administration both advocated the Bosnian and Serbian interventions and tried to broker the deal that would have given the Palestinians their own state. 'They do not know that five hundred Muslims died in the World Trade Center, something strictly forbidden by the Koran... And they do not know that when the FBI asked for two hundred Arabic speakers to translate, there were fifteen thousand applications.'

The war is with the most extreme sects of ultra-fundamentalist Islam, represented by the Taliban and Al Qaeda, the ones that oppress their own people, keep them uneducated and poor; who believe that all you need to know of life can be found by memorising one ancient book (of course, this is a belief not restricted to fundamentalists of the Muslim persuasion alone); who don't even teach their (male) children the alphabet or mathematics or the scientific method, but indoctrinate them with propaganda, including the belief, taught in some Pakistani ultra-religious madrassahs, that America and the Jews have created genetically engineered dinosaurs for the purpose of eating good Muslim children. Such things would be ridiculous and laughable, if not for the consequences of this type of 'education' for the rest of the striving world, much of which looks longingly at America and sees there something to like.

This is a book about American products and styles; about American psychology, genres and trends. It's about Starbucks and P Diddy, Shaq and John Wayne – and about Barbie-doll blondes with big silicone breasts.

It's a book about the psychic and physical spaces that allow for good old American outrageousness, from PT Barnum to the two gay lovers in New York's Central Park, a teenage boy and a pre-operative transsexual, who, one fine spring day, took off all their clothes and climbed high into the branches of a tree. For four hours they refused police pleas to come down, please, and instead put on 'an X-rated sex spectacle' in their 'unlikely love nest fifty feet above' the park, as one of the several New York newspapers that covered the event so breathlessly reported.

'We don't get this back home', exclaimed one of the many tourists transfixed by the spectacle, while another said, 'We were going to go to the Empire State Building, but we thought we'd stay here instead.'

And when the two gay lovers finally did come down from their perch in the tree, they faced perhaps a fine and maybe even a night or two in jail for their escapade, but the state of New York would not punish them in any way for their sexual orientation or religious persuasion, which is not the case in many other parts of the world.

In America, gay people get their own their TV network, targeted especially to them, because they're regarded, ultimately, as just another group of consumers worth pursuing; in America, young women who aspire to be surgeons and astronauts have their role models and career paths, and young women who aspire to be Barbie-doll blondes with big silicon breasts can try out for avidly watched TV shows that will pay for their cosmetic surgery. *Baywatch* may be off the air now, but in America there is no end to sexy 'jiggle' shows, or of audiences eager to watch them. You may disagree, you may be offended by the 'bad taste' of some parts of the popular culture, but in America the off switch is always in your own hands.

America is always changing, always up to the moment but the core values to which it aspires remain the same. After all, not so long ago, a little anti-Semitism or casual anti-Negro slurs were acceptable, even in polite society. But, unlike many other parts of the world, in America there is the possibility of social progress and of righting a long-standing societal wrong.

America is not yet perfect, but it is the land of striving, where progress can be made. And if you doubt that's true, consider the reaction to the alleged slur that Princess Michael of Kent delivered to a boisterous group of accomplished young urban Black professionals, whom she meant to rebuke for their noisiness at the next table in a restaurant in New York's Greenwich Village, where she was supping. The Princess demanded quiet, the diners said, slamming her hand down on their adjoining table. 'You need to go back to the colonies!' she supposedly snapped, though she later denied the remark.

Were the young African-American diners intimidated? Did they forthwith quiet down?

Quite the opposite. They got even noisier, according to reports. After all, they were the regulars at the restaurant, not the Princess, who was escorted – fuming, we are told – to another table far away.

'Maybe I've been lucky, but I've never run into that kind of racism in my life,' one of the diners, a publicist, told the *New York Post*.

Nothing could be more American than talking back and standing firm in the face of someone with a powerful hereditary prerogative.

It's one of the grand pillars the country is built upon, and it's still what Americans teach their children in school. Be rude and condescending to Americans at your peril, because Americans will talk right back.

In every generation, many American kids 'get' it, are embued with that basic understanding of America's democratic core values. And if you doubt it, consider this: in up-to-the-moment pre-teen and young-teen American kid talk, the newest word to express the old idea of being hopelessly 'unhip' or 'uncool' is...

Burka.

As in, 'That's just so burka, dude!'

So, boys and girls, slip off your \$175 (£110) Air Jordan high tops, kick back with your Big Macs and Cokes, put on some rock 'n' roll (or hip-hop, or jazz, or country-and-western music). And fire up the old 'puter and surf the Web, where a universe of pornography is just a mouse click away, where you can troll a chat room and talk to White boys from Norway who sound just like Black kids from Harlem.

Or maybe you want to throw on a DVD. Go ahead, watch a classic film noir from the '40s, a special-effects blockbuster or just click over to cable for some 24-7 real-time war news.

How about a nice quiet evening with a good book? Maybe a hard-boiled detective story or the latest self-help bestseller. Perhaps a dieting guide, or a guide to working out and the health culture.

Your jeans may have been sewn in Thailand and your computer constructed in Taiwan. But when it comes to pop culture, odds are, whatever it was, it was truly made – or made-over – by America. And if you turn the page, you will learn some of the reasons why.

A word of caution: how and why much of the world came to dream American is not a linear story and, accordingly, this is not a linear book. So be ready to play the ancient children's game thought to have been taken to Britain by the Romans, which then, in the era of the Empire, exported it to the rest of the world.

Ready, set...

Hopscotch!

1 Mad Ave Sells America
(And The Rest Of The World Eagerly Buys)

What killed Soviet-style communism? Did the American government's steely resolve bring that ugly concrete wall dividing Berlin down, or was it really American popular culture and American rock 'n' roll?

And why didn't it work when the US government enlisted a veteran of the Madison Avenue advertising wars to 'sell America' to the Muslim world in the aftermath of 9-11? After all, who can match Mad Ave when it comes to selling Coke, Pepsi, Big Macs and big movies?

In the wake of September 11, American political and civic leaders expressed not only anger but consternation: it was now brutally clear that not everyone in the rest of the big, wide world loves America. 'Why do they hate us?' became for a time a plaintive cry of politicos and pundits across the land.

The first, reflexive answer they came up with was, well, typically American in a corporate, bureaucratic sort of way. It must be because, said Washington's perplexed pundits and solons...

The rest of world doesn't understand the brand!

And so, forthwith, the American government installed Charlotte Beers, a Madison Avenue veteran originally from Beaumont, Texas, as Under Secretary of State for Public Diplomacy and Public Affairs. She had once done market research for Uncle Ben's Rice, before rising to become head of advertising giants J Walter Thompson and Ogilvy & Mather, and was generally regarded as the most powerful woman ever in American advertising.

In her new State Department job, she was tasked with the mission of 'selling' the American 'brand' to the seething, hostile, impoverished masses of the Muslim world. Madison Avenue sells to 'targets', whether those targets are, say, teenage girls, 30-something mothers or, in this case, the hundreds of millions of Muslims who live in hopelessness and poverty and are oppressed and exploited by brutal oligarchies and dictatorships. The target audience, in short, was the wretched of the earth, Muslim-style, from among whose dispossessed ranks had come the desperados who had been persuaded by fiery Imams that the better way to better themselves and improve their people's lot was to return to the values of the 13th century, that the enemy was far-away America, which wanted their oil and to sell them stuff, and not, say, the local nabobs with their slippers firmly on their people's neck.

The 9-11 hijackers sought glory by sacrificing themselves, by massacring the women and children of their enemies, and they were regarded as heroes by too many in the Muslim lands.

Selling Uncle Sam to the masses in the Muslim 'street', who might better be given their daily portions of Uncle Ben's, along with a real education, turned out to be not so simple.

Ms Beers set about producing 'image' spots, portraying the USA as a paradise of multicultural tolerance, where Muslims could practise their religion peacefully and live with Jews, Christians and Buddhists in peace and harmony. She also produced a glossy booklet, entitled 'The Mosques of America'.

It was sanctimonious and it was transparently propaganda, and despite its $15 million budget her campaign didn't work. In early 2003, less than two months before Ms Beers returned to the private sector, during an interview on American public television, she herself pointed to some of the reasons why the propaganda campaign had failed.

For one thing, 'there's a great belief in Muslim countries that the whole lifestyle of our country and its way of being is decadent, faithless, and therefore not a proper environment for one who wants to practice their Islam religion,' Ms Beers said, adding that of course that wasn't the case, that, 'Muslim families in this country are thriving. They have an exceptional growth rate. They have the most beautiful mosques. They have their own schools, as they like. They live a very typical American life.'

For another, despite getting her radio and TV image spots on air in Malaysia, Indonesia, Pakistan and Kuwait during a 'high-television viewing period' – that is, during Ramadan, the month-long Islamic holiday period – the Muslim viewers were, as she put it, a 'little dubious about who's sending them this message, a little skeptical'.

And that was partly, of course, because the spots themselves were US State Department funded and, therefore, suspect by their very nature. But even more importantly than that, most governments in the Muslim world, even the ostensible allies of America, which invariably kept a tight rein on their homegrown media, too, simply declined to air the spots. Surprise, surprise.

Of course, the American government, which had begun its own counter-propaganda broadcasts into Nazi-occupied Europe in World War II with the Voice of America and had continued broadcasting behind the Iron Curtain during the Cold War with Radio Free Europe and Radio Free Liberty, knew how to deal with that. The government created Radio Sawa (Radio Together), a 24-hour, 7-day FM radio network broadcasting throughout the Middle East.

The music, including hip-hop and techno mixed with both local Arabic and American pop sounds, was wildly popular with the kids on the Arab street, who turned out to like Britney Spears and pop music with an infectious beat as much as anyone. But, as commentators on all sides of the political spectrum have noted, the kids tended to dismiss the two, ten-minute Radio Sawa news broadcasts every hour as nothing but propaganda.

'Most people I have talked to agree that it's nice to have the music, but that the news is a bit of a joke,' is how Ali Abunimah, vice-president of the Arab-American Action Network, put it. Of course, the 'news' on most of the Middle East government-approved local newscasts was of strikingly dubious usefulness, and a bit of a sad joke, too. The truth is, real freedom of the press – here, there and everywhere – requires multiple news sources, reflecting multiple interests and perspectives.

But what of the inflammatory imagery of injured children and destroyed homes that the Arab satellite networks were broadcasting throughout the Middle East? 'Change the channel,' a hard-nosed American general sniffed.

The Beers initiative seemed to confuse propaganda with advertising and Madison Avenue and Hollywood values with national policy and Washington DC. In fact, it wasn't the first time this had happened. In the run-up to the first Gulf War in 1991, after Saddam Hussein's Iraq invaded Kuwait but before the start of the war that was called Desert Storm, the United States government 'undertook to produce a film', according to former Ambassador William A Rugh, the president and chief executive officer of America-Mideast Educational and Training Services (AMIDEAST), a nonprofit organisation promoting cooperation between Americans and the people of the Middle East.

'The purpose of the film was to demonstrate the overwhelming power of the United States and the coalition that was arrayed against Saddam Hussein and to persuade Saddam and his advisers to withdraw from Kuwait without a conflict,' said Mr Rugh, also the former US Ambassador to the Republic of Yemen and the United Arab Emirates.

And while that didn't exactly work, you can't fault the American government for trying. It's what governments always do. After all, did not American propaganda even play its part in 1776, in the War of American Independence? Wasn't the American Revolution the 'first in history based on evaporating brand loyalty' – to British tea and other consumer goods, as Northwestern University historian TH Breen contends in his recent book, *The Marketplace of Revolution: How Consumer Politics Shaped American Independence*. And wasn't the first master salesman of the competing new American 'brand' none other than Benjamin Franklin? 'American colonists made sure their version of battles with British troops arrived in England before the official dispatches from the British field commanders,' according to Edwin J Feulner, the president of The Heritage Foundation, a well-known and conservatively oriented Washington think-tank. Benjamin Franklin, who was in London from 1765 to 1775 as the American colonies' 'unofficial' ambassador, 'made sure the colonists' accounts were spread far and wide, defusing the impact of official reports which often arrived days later,' Mr Feulner said. It's a tactic that's been adopted by rebels right up to the present day: make certain that the citizens of the enemy homeland are well acquainted with your message and point of view, and with the inevitability of your eventual triumph.

Now flash forward some 214 years. It is now 9 November 1989. The Berlin Wall has stood for more than a quarter of a century as the very symbol of a divided Europe and of the prison that is drab, regimented, Soviet-style Communism. Behind that wall languishes half of Europe. But today the wall is falling. Remarkably though, there are no NATO tanks punching through its concrete. No flights of bombers assaulting it from the air. There are no steel-tipped armies of the West massing to knock it down.

No, the Wall is being brought down from the East, by the East Germans themselves who have taken to the street demanding their share of The Dream, the one that they can hear about and see.

The Dream is wafting in on the airwaves from the West. And that means that, despite attempts at electronic jamming and censorship, the comrades of East Germany and eastern Europe know all about not only Coke and McDonald's, but about *Dallas* and *Dynasty*, two American prime-time TV soap operas of the 1980s. Understandably, though intellectually they may know better, the struggling proletariat – bereft of consumer goods and trapped on the wrong side of the Wall – tends to take these glossy Hollywood-produced melodramas as social-realist documentaries of the good life.

And the East know all about rock 'n' roll, too. When the dam finally breaks and the East Germans are free to rush West, the first things they ask for are oranges, which they are amazed to find are plentiful, and records – mostly pop music or rock.

In the West, on both sides of the generation gap, rock – which once was viewed by the older generation with horror as the triumph of licentiousness and the End of Civilisation As We Know It – has come to be accepted. Now, on both sides of the Wall, rock 'n' roll stands for the triumph of freedom and personal expression, not to mention for unfettered sexuality. And on both sides of the Wall, they know about David Hasselhoff, too…

These days, perhaps not everyone remembers what a worldwide force for Americanism Mister Hasselhoff once was, and that was even before *Baywatch*. In that programme he starred as 'Mitch Buchannon' – chief lifeguard by day and, later, private detective by night in the execrable and mercifully short-lived spin-off, *Baywatch Nights*. Even more than *Charlie's Angels*, its predecessor in the fevered affections of teenage boys, *Baywatch* was arguably the apogee of the so-called 'jiggle show' gracing TV sets all around the globe with a succession of young, Barbie Doll-perfect model/actresses, all playing trim and athletic LA lifeguards with names like 'Shauni' (Erika Eleniak), 'Lani' (Carmen Electra) and 'CJ' (Pamela Anderson).

Of course, the show invariably found some opportunity in each and every episode to display the women in all their leggy glory, wearing their high-cut thigh, skimpy, one-piece red bathing suits, and running in slow motion along the beaches of southern California.

Baywatch, which was just getting underway in the fraught year that Communism was collapsing, only lasted two seasons on an American network, but, later, in international syndication, it became the most-watched TV show on the planet in the 1990s.

More than just a square jaw, a clear eye and a full head of hair, Mister Hasselhoff was a man of parts, talent and personal charm, and like many an actor before him he realised – as early as *Knight Rider*, the pre-*Baywatch* hit series in which he starred alongside a talking car – that simply acting was, well, simply not enough. Like John Tesh, the one-time Ken-doll *Entertainment Tonight* anchor, who surprised his scoffing non-fans because it turned out that he could really play a light-jazz repertoire on the piano, Mr Hasselhoff really could sing. Eventually, he even appeared on Broadway. And though he was disparaged in the United States, he became a soft-rock sensation in Europe, particularly in Germany, ancestral home of his forebears.

By that pivotal summer of 1989, his song 'Looking For Freedom', an English-language cover of a German hit from the 1970s, was a Euro-hit, and it became something of an anthem for the giant crowds gathered to protest the privations of eastern Europe locked behind the Iron Curtain.

And so it was that on New Year's Eve, less than two months after the Wall was first breached, it was none other than the Man from Baywatch who stood atop the concrete ruins of the Berlin Wall. 'Close to a million East and West German fans stood together in the freezing cold at midnight watching me perform,' he told the BBC. 'I was overcome with emotion.'

Of Hollywood it is said that there are more Men of the Year than there are days of the year. And it is simple truth that Tinseltown's swollen egos are more often the true excuse for its bulging social calendar, rather than any desire to put on a tuxedo and raise money for some truly needy charity while paying $1,000 (£625) a plate for dinner. Not that even pampered A-list Hollywood denizens don't have an innocent and idealistic side; they do want to be seen as being on the side of the angels and doing good. And of course the publicity doesn't hurt.

So it is not surprising that in Hollywood's trumpeting self-regard, it wasn't only the Berlin Wall and Soviet-style Communism that fell to its irresistible blandishments. Hollywood brought down the apartheid government of South Africa, too.

Well, yes, Nelson Mandela did have something to do with it. But don't forget that seminal moment in the recording studio when America's Influentials – its premiere rock, pop, reggae and rap stars – all banded together in the mid-'80s to vow they would not play South Africa's Sun City resort until the apartheid system of segregation was gone. Now there was a blow right where it mattered: a direct hit to the bank account of the South African tourist industry.

Then, later in that same decade, *The Cosby Show* went to South Africa television. And that, many in Hollywood will tell you, was the decisive act.

The hit NBC half-hour situation comedy series was the most popular show on American television in the second half of the 1980s. It depicted a middle-class Black two-parent family with five children in the very same idealised way that had once been reserved exclusively for White families on American television, in TV's own Whites Only days. Cosby was 'Doctor Heathcliff "Cliff" Huxtable', an obstetrician/gynaecologist, and Phylicia Rashad was his wife 'Clair', a successful attorney.

The Cosby Show was an expertly played 'Father Knows Best'-style series, promulgating sterling, middle-class, pro-social messages and values. It was heart-warming, goofy and sweetly funny, too.

When the programme began to air on South Africa television, South Africans of all colours could at last tune in and see this idealised racial equality right on their home screens. And there, too, as it was everywhere else it was shown around the world, the show was a Number-One must-see TV hit. And, in due course, apartheid fell...

Modern advertising, according to historian David Potter, is 'peculiarly identified with American abundance'. In an economy of scarcity 'advertising is not badly needed', he said in *People Of Plenty: Economic Abundance And The American Character*, his influential 1954 work, because everyone sells or consumes what they produce. 'It's only when supply outstrips demand that the need for advertising really begins.'

But of course, advertising creates demand too, and not just among those who can afford to buy what it is that advertising tempts them to crave. Advertising 'appeals primarily to the desires, the wants – cultivated or natural – of the individual, and it sometimes offers as its goal a power to command the envy of others by outstripping them in the consumption of goods and services', as Professor Potter also observed.

A half century ago, when Professor Potter penned these insights, the world was a different place. Europe was still busy recovering from the devastations of World War II and was divided physically by ideology. The Cold War was underway. In Africa, the post-colonial era was just beginning. In Indochina, the epic battle of Dien Bien Phu was being fought, and soon the French would lose their South Asian colony. In the United States, until the middle of that year, when the Supreme Court decided the Brown Versus The Board of Education case, the home-grown apartheid of 'separate but equal' was still the law of the land.

Elvis on *Ed Sullivan* was still two years off, and the 'youth culture' was still years away. Media had yet to proliferate. Television, which already was becoming ubiquitous, was then a small, snowy, black-and-white screen in a boxy wooden cabinet (although the first colour sets were manufactured that year, selling for $1,000 [£625], then a princely sum).

The new home medium was wildly popular from its earliest beginnings, thanks in no small part to a red-headed comedienne named Lucy and her apoplectic Cuban husband Ricky. A year earlier, in January 1953, the 'Birth of Little Ricky' episode of *I Love Lucy* was watched by 44 million people (nearly 72 per cent of all Americans tuned into television at the time), creating the first must-see sensation of the television age.

Back then, there were no such things as mobile phones, personal computers, cyberspace or the Internet. All were inconceivable or, at best, merely woolly science-fiction dreams.

But even back then, in that long ago mid-20th-century world, there was Coca-Cola, and Pepsi too. There was General Motors, Mobil Oil, Kellogg's, Levi's, Timex and a host of other internationally known brands. Each name was more famous in almost every corner of the world than just about anything comparable that was locally produced.

In fact as recently as the turn of the millennium, the most recognised and admired brand name in South Africa, half a world away from the United States, was Coca-Cola, the soft drink formulated in Atlanta, Georgia, which the South African *Sunday Times* called a 'national icon'. Coke is a national icon on both sides of the Atlantic, too, rated among the country's top ten 'best' brands in both the US and the UK.

South Africans drink more Coke than any other soft drink, the South African *Sunday Times* reported, and they 'admire' it more than any local brand. Why? 'Years of successful locally flavoured advertising and wide participation in community life – from sports sponsorships and sports development to entrepreneurial and education projects,' the *Times* opined.

That was the mantra of Madison Avenue, too. 'Before you can have a share of market, you must have a share of mind,' as Chicago adman Leo Burnett famously said in the mid-1950s. Market-by-market localism, with its high-profile good works and careful consideration of local tastes, turned out to be the key to creating a successful international brand.

That's as true in Bombay as it is in Brooklyn, and that's the reason that the top names on Madison Avenue are the top names in advertising in Europe and on the Indian subcontinent, too. In the '90s, in a period of consolidation and conglomeration, the ad game in India was internationalised, just as it was almost everywhere else. Today, every major name on Madison Avenue, including the Interpublic Group, Omnicom, Publicis and WPP, is also a presence in Bombay, often as the majority owner of a prominent Indian agency.

Consider just this partial itinerary from one recent year in the life of a senior Madison Avenue executive, Joe Uva, the peripatetic chief executive of OMD Worldwide (who is also the architect of the single largest deal in the history of American television advertising, a one-year, $1 billion agreement between his agency and the Walt Disney Company): four trips from New York to Asia, including stops in Korea, Taiwan, Japan, Hong Kong and Singapore. Four trips to Europe, including visits to the United Kingdom, France, Spain and Italy. Two trips to Canada. One to Australia. Imagine the frequent flyer miles!

It doesn't hurt to have a catchy slogan and a nice tune to help sell a brand, and that's also where Madison Avenue comes in. Remember 'Things Go Better With Coke'? How about 'Coke – It's The Real Thing'? Or the little tune that goes 'I'd Like To Buy The World A Coke'? All of those, and many more, are the product of one Mad Ave mind, that of former McCann-Erickson vice-president Ike Herbert, who left the Madison

Avenue agency in the '60s to join the client side at Coca-Cola. By the time of his retirement a quarter of a century later, he was Coke's chief marketing officer, and the man widely regarded as responsible for turning Coke into a brand known in every corner of the world.

The slogans, tunes and corporate symbols have become, in effect, an international language. Hum Coke's ubiquitous 'I'd Like To Buy The World' ditty in almost any corner of the globe and you're likely to get a smile of recognition. Increasingly, the same is true of many other American brands. Try it, for example, with 'Priceless', Mastercard's latest slogan, or 'It takes a lickin', but it keeps on tickin',' the Timex Watches slogan from way back in the 1950s. That memorable little slogan is one of the big reasons that, at the turn of the millennium, the watch company that had been around since the middle of the 19th century was the most recognisable brand name in all of American fashion.

Tastes great? 'Have a Coke and a smile,' as Ike Herbert would say. Sure, but the good opinion a majority of South Africans – not to mention Europeans – have of a sugary American soft drink first formulated as a headache tonic in 1886 is no accident of taste. Actually, in the case of the Europeans anyway, it was originally a fortune of war. Girding the American Expeditionary Forces of World War II in their titanic struggle with the dark legions of Nazism were no fewer than 64 portable Coca-Cola bottling plants. They were dispatched to the far-flung war fronts by Coke's legendary president Robert Woodruff, who not only thought it his patriotic duty to make sure the soldiers and sailors had his nickel soda pop ready to hand on the battlefield, but who also oversaw the introduction of the six-pack, the proliferation of the original brand and its subsequent worldwide expansion. By the end of the war, according to one estimate, five billion Cokes had been guzzled by the troops.

When peace came at last, the plants remained dug in, and Coke's flag stayed planted in the war-torn European soil. Later, of course, the forces of Coke were joined on the ground by their biggest American ally of the second half of the 20th century: McDonald's.

In the 19th century it was said that the sun never set on the British Empire. At the beginning of the 21st, the sun never sets on the Golden Arches, where some 29,000 meals are sold every minute at more than 27,000 restaurants in 119 countries.

Though McDonald's itself consumes five per cent of the potato crop and two per cent of all chickens raised in the United States, the majority of its profits come from its international operations, which overwhelmingly consist of local franchises staffed locally. And that is one secret of its success.

Outside the United States, the familiar Big Mac and fries is supplemented by such locally appealing fare as the Maharaj Mac (a lamb Mac, in Bombay), the McArabia (a chicken sandwich on Arabian-style bread, in the Middle East), the McCafe (in Vienna), corn soup (Tokyo), rice (Jakarta) yoghurt-style cheese (Brazil) and roast pork (Seoul).

In both Russia and China, where the Golden Arches were first raised in 1990, McDonald's is regarded as a bastion of cleanliness and reliability. In the United States, when fast food diets became implicated in the epidemic of obesity, and 'health' became the new dietary watchword, causing McDonald's sales to lag, the company responded by adding upscale offerings, including panini, salads and low-carb foods, to its menu. The result: sales shot right back up.

Perhaps you'd like a DVD or a free music download with those fries? Fear not, it's on the way. McDonald's is currently testing out in-stores kiosks stocked with DVDs for rent. It has also launched a partnership with Sony offering customers in five countries (the US, the UK, Canada, France and Germany) a free song download from Sony's website.

When the complaints about fast food being a factor in the national and international obesity epidemics reached a crescendo, it wasn't only McDonald's management that was prepared to take action. An unknown independent documentary filmmaker was ready with his credit cards and was also prepared to put his body on the line for his art. Maxing out credits cards to finance a first film started out as a rite of passage for aspiring independent filmmakers, but now it has become almost a cliché, and each year's Sundance Film Festival wouldn't be complete without some heartfelt tale of passionate auteurial commitment expressed in overdrafts and credit binges. So when young filmmaker Morgan Spurlock, a graduate of New York University's film school, got the brainstorm to document what would happen if he subsisted on nothing but fast food for a month, the first thing he did was reach for the plastic, using eight different credit cards to finance his production company.

In *Super Size Me* (2004), a favourite on the festival circuit, which he directed as well as stars in, Spurlock travels the country, from Golden Arches to Golden Arches, subsisting on nothing but Big Macs, Egg McMuffins and the like. He conducts person-on-the-street interviews and consults with medical experts. And as the experiment continues, he steadily gains weight and his cholesterol and blood pressure go up. At the beginning of the film, Spurlock weighs 84kg (185lb). After a month of eating only fast food, Spurlock's weight is up to 95kg (210lb).

One reviewer, not untypically, called the picture 'effective agitprop – effective enough that McDonald's announced it was discontinuing the Super-Size option shortly after its Sundance premiere'. Another reviewer was not so impressed. The movie is a 'prime example of an all-American sport', wrote Peter Rainer, the chairman of the National Society of Film Critics, 'making a spectacle of yourself for fun and profit'. And for that matter, he added, who wouldn't gain weight on a 5,000-calorie-a-day diet and no exercise? The director 'could have achieved much the same dire results dining exclusively at high-end French eateries'.

Of course, the fast-food chain took quick action to protect its image. It closely guards its image as a caring corporation, and has a long history of doing well by doing good, particularly with its charitable Ronald McDonald houses. These are homes near children's hospitals where parents of children being treated for serious or life-threatening diseases can go and stay close to their children. The children themselves can expect cheering appearances by Ronald McDonald, the familiar clown in the orange fright wig who is the corporation's symbol. Currently there are some 200 Ronald McDonald houses worldwide, in more than 30 countries.

When Joan Kroc, the widow of McDonald's corporate founder, died in 2003 she left $1.5 billion to the Salvation Army, which was just one of the many charities to benefit (for example, America's perennially cash-strapped National Public Radio got $200 million). It was the largest single charitable bequest ever made by an individual to a single institution.

The founder of McDonald's, Ray Kroc, died in 1984, but he lived long enough to see the little San Bernadino, California, hamburger business he bought in 1961 from the Donald brothers, Michael and Maurice (who went by the nickname 'Mac'), turn into a multibillion dollar international empire.

Ray was a 'brand zealot', whose mantra was 'Quality, Service, Cleanliness, and Value', *Fortune* magazine once said of him. 'He'd show up unannounced, and the next thing you knew, this guy in a tailor-made suit's picking up disposed napkins on the street,' the McDonald's manager who thought up the Egg McMuffin told the magazine. Another McDonald's executive recalled him peering through binoculars at a nearby McDonald's drive-through line, to see how business was being done.

It was Ray Kroc's genius to franchise the McDonald's standardised hamburger-making production-line techniques all around the country, and then all around the world. To that end, the company even maintains a Hamburger University campus near Chicago, where managers can graduate with a Bachelor of Hamburgerology degree.

Today, some 80 per cent of the McDonald's franchises around the world are locally owned (and virtually all are locally staffed). The company now derives some 60 per cent of its profits from its international operations. So ubiquitous is the Big Mac that no less than *The Economist* has taken to employing it as a convenient measure of whether or not one national currency is at the proper exchange rate with another. The magazine calculates what it calls the Big Mac Index (BMI). The BMI compares the cost of a Big Mac in one country in its local currency to that of a Big Mac in a second country in that country's local currency. The ratio between the two is then compared to the actual exchange rate between the two currencies to see whether one of the currencies is over- or undervalued.

When James Cantalupo, McDonald's 60-year-old chief executive officer, collapsed and died of a sudden heart attack in spring 2004, he was replaced by Charlie Bell, a 43-year-old Australian, who became the company's sixth CEO and its first to come from outside the United States.

So emblematic of globalisation has the fast-food company become, in fact, that multi-Pulitzer Prize-winning *New York Times* columnist Tom Friedman once even proposed a McDonald's Axiom, which he called 'The Golden Arches Theory Of Conflict Prevention'. The theory proposed that no two countries with a McDonald's franchise would ever go to war with each other. Thus far, that 'rule' has been broken once: when the American Air Force bombed Belgrade in the late 1990s to force the end of ethnic cleansing in Kosovo and Bosnia.

But perhaps the ultimate accolade to the ultimate all-American meal, a burger with fries, is the following famous bit of arch and witty dialogue from *Pulp Fiction* (1994), Quentin Tarantino's darkly comic noir masterpiece. Jules (Samuel Jackson) and Vincent (John Travolta), two hit men on a mission to recover a mysteriously glowing suitcase, are driving in a car, when Vincent, apropos of absolutely nothing at all, asks Jules if he knows what they call a Quarter Pounder with cheese in Paris.

'They don't call it a Quarter Pounder with cheese?' Jules replies.

'No man, they got the metric system. They wouldn't know what the fuck a Quarter Pounder is.'

'Then what do they call it?'

'They call it a Royale with cheese.'

'A Royale with cheese. What do they call a Big Mac?'

'A Big Mac's a Big Mac, but they call it Le Big Mac.'

'Le Big Mac? Ha-ha-ha-ha. What do they call a Whopper?'

'I dunno. I didn't go into Burger King.'

Meanwhile, a decade later and back in the Middle East, things were becoming more difficult for big, recognisable corporate American symbols, even those that sold tasty fast food. One McDonald's was torched in Saudi Arabia, another in Lebanon was bombed. Fundamentalists called for boycotts of all things American, and especially of all things American that also happened to do business in Israel.

On the other hand, there was all that chewy-good food and all that fizzy Coca-Cola to drink. And there was that relentless McDonald's all-American optimism and its emphasis on localism, which in the Middle East has produced not only the chicken McArabia, but the McFelafel in Egypt.

'There is no liaison between the McArabia and politics,' a McDonald's franchisee in Dubai declared, sounding all-

Americanly optimistic himself as he pronounced the sandwich a big hit. 'It's a local taste finder, like the McFelafel in Egypt.'

In Egypt, where the first Golden Arches arrived a decade ago, there are now more than 50 McDonald's, with more than 3,000 employees, and the company reports that more than 90 per cent of the raw materials used for its restaurants in Egypt are 'sourced locally'.

In Saudi Arabia, where the first McDonald's opened in 1993, there are now 71 restaurants, including 2 in the holy city of Mecca.

In Israel, where the first McDonald's also opened in 1993, there are now more than 80 outlets, employing more than 3,000 locals, and the company reports that it gets 'over eighty per cent of its ingredients locally, including one-hundred-per cent kosher beef patties'.

By comparison, in Japan there are more than 3,000 McDonald's.

In all three Middle East countries, as in Japan and elsewhere, the fast-food chain itself does good works locally, associating itself particularly with charities that benefit children.

A disavowal of any possible political connotation to the McArabia notwithstanding, how is American popular culture doing in the over-heated, politicised and polarised world of the Middle Eastern street? Who will win the battle for Middle Eastern hearts and minds – the oil sheiks or the chocolate shakes?

A solution at the point of a gun is one thing. Perhaps the most extreme of the Islamic fundamentalists will actually win and eventually there will even be a caliphate, some throwback Islamic transnational state in which Shariah is all, and fast food is just a dim memory crowded out by rote chanting.

Perhaps the various 'knock-off' products of famous American brands being touted these days to Muslims throughout the Middle East will fare better than their Iron Curtain counterparts did in the old days of the Evil Empire.

Perhaps America's more obtuse and benighted political leaders will so totally alienate the rest of the world that the yummy taste of an American burger, fries and coke will yet turn to ashes in the international customer's mouth.

Until then though, the smart money should be on the persuasive powers of the Coke and the Big Mac, not to mention the grey flannel forces of the internationalised Mad Ave.

'The fact of the matter is that Arab and Muslim societies are already Westernised/Americanised in profound ways,' according to an editorial in a recent edition of *Al-Ahram*, the influential Egyptian weekly newspaper. 'Indeed, the past few years – the same years which have witnessed a record number of American flag burnings on Arab streets – have seen an amazingly swift Americanisation of the Arab world.

'In Cairo, *Friends*-inspired Central Perk-style coffee houses have been proliferating like mushrooms… The American sit-com, itself, is probably as popular in Arab middle-class households as it is in the US… And when exactly did Valentine's Day become an Egyptian national holiday, let alone a Palestinian and pan-Arab one?' the editorialist asked.

The *Al-Ahram* editorial also took note of the rise of American-style multiplexes showing the latest American films, the proliferation of satellite dishes playing the latest episodes of *Frasier* and international MTV and the ubiquity of the Internet among Egyptian youth. 'Simply put, not just Western culture, but also a distinctly American culture, is as integral to modern culture in Egypt as it is to the rest of the Arab world…. And just like the American people, we get heaps of garbage and quite a few gems.'

Sound familiar? It will on Madison Avenue, where they invented modern Valentine's Day, as well as any number of clever, eye-catching schemes, memorable slogans and compulsively hummable tunes, many of them known worldwide and some that just should be. For example, a few years ago, one clever advertising man pitching to get the account of Pepsi-Cola, Coke's biggest competitor, came up with the brainstorm to paint all of the round manhole covers in Manhattan, the media capital of the world, to look just like the red, white and blue Pepsi logo. As it happened, New York, ever in need of new sources of revenue, agreed to the scheme, but, unfathomably, Pepsi's marketing executives turned the adman's idea down.

Maybe they thought it would be undignified to have the polyglot crowds of Manhattan stepping all over their corporate logo. Perhaps they thought it would somehow be like Saddam Hussein displaying a mosaic of George Bush the Elder's face on the floor at the entrance to Baghdad's al-Rashid hotel, forcing all who entered to walk upon his visage.

Then again, maybe the adman was just ahead of his time. Nowadays of course, Americans are busily putting brand logos on just about everything, from covering every inch of NASCAR racers and drivers' uniforms to advertising on the backs of Kentucky Derby jockeys. Even the so-called National Pastime is not exempt: advertising logos for *Spider-Man 2*, a summer 2004 Hollywood special-effects blockbuster from Sony-owned Columbia Pictures, were scheduled to be plastered atop bases at 15 major league ballparks during major-league games one summer weekend. The teams themselves would divide up a bonanza – around $4 million (£2.5 million), according to reports.

It's tempting to think that finding new places to decorate with advertising is actually the new national pastime. But seemingly there are limits. Just one day after the base-covering scheme was announced by the press, a whirlwind of protest from fans forced MLB and Columbia to back away. But by then, of course, they'd also hit a grand-slam home run of free publicity.

From the autumn of 2004, tourists in Midtown Manhattan will be able to stroll over to 50th and Madison for a look at the five best advertising slogans of all time. They are scheduled to be displayed, along with the five best advertising icons, Hollywood Walk of Fame-style, on the first ever Advertising Walk of Fame.

Who gets to decide which are the best? The public, of course, online. How many of these finalists for a place on the Walk of Fame do you remember?...

'Don't leave home without it' (American Express)
'Think different' (Apple)
'The ultimate driving machine' (BMW)
'Whassup?' (Budweiser)
'Look Ma, no cavities' (Crest)
'A diamond is forever' (DeBeers)
'We bring good things to life' (General Electric)
'When you care enough to send the very best' (Hallmark Cards)
'Melts in your mouth, not in your hands' (M&M's)
'You deserve a break today!' (McDonald's)
'Tastes great, less filling' (Miller)
'Just do it' (Nike)
'It takes a lickin', but it keeps on tickin'' (Timex)
'Fly the friendly skies' (United Airlines)
'You've come a long way, baby' (Virginia Slims)
'Where's the beef?' (Wendy's)
'Let your fingers do the walking' (Yellow Pages)

And among the finalists for best advertising icon, which includes characters such as the Energizer Bunny, the Jolly Green Giant, the Michelin Man and the Pillsbury Dough Boy, is, of course, Ronald McDonald.

Despite the best efforts of the terrorists, the despots and the oligarches, American popular culture continues to flood into the Middle East, just as it once flooded across the Iron Curtain. It is an article of Madison Avenue faith that share of market follows share of mind; and on that basis, the prospects for American pop culture are looking good.

Madison Avenue can be expected to sloganeer and shine it all up, just as it does elsewhere, in the interests of getting those Middle Eastern cash registers to ring. And in the process of selling a few Whoppers, you might expect that Mad Ave will even tell a whopper or two, though, one hopes, nothing on the order of genetically altered dinosaurs.

Truth is the best advertisement, even in wartime and even when the truth is ugly. Most Americans know that. And most Americans are horrified by the still-evolving story of young American soldiers abusing Iraqi captives in the very prison, Abu Ghraib, west of Baghdad, where Saddam Hussein was said to have inflicted the most cruel and inhumane tortures against his opponents.

War is ugly business, but there are rules of conduct. And the difference between the dictatorship and the democracy is that no one inside Iraq dared to speak out against the dictator, while in America wrong actions are examined and criticised openly.

When the American administration declared its intention to summarily tear the infamous prison down, a military judge stepped in to stop the planned demolition, declaring that Abu Ghraib was a crime scene and couldn't be touched until after the soldiers' trials. War is ugly business; it would be uglier still without America's competing power centres and institutionalised checks and balances.

Early indications are that the abuses were committed by young reservists – that is, part-time soldiers – who were shipped off to war without being specifically trained in the proper and permissible procedures for guarding prisoners of war or running a prison. Whether the abuses stemmed from a particular policy, or some coercive interrogation philosophy, or how far up the chain of command responsibility for such actions goes – all this remains to be determined. We do know that in America wrong actions by some Americans in uniform have been brought to light and publicly condemned by other Americans, including other Americans in uniform, who can speak out without fear of ending up in some dark jail themselves.

This shameful episode was also brought to light in the usual American way, by a free press and by a few brave individual Americans who spoke out against injustice. And one of the very first in-depth accounts about the scandal inside the Iraqi prison came from Seymour Hersh, the very same journalist who, in November 1969, broke the story of the My Lai massacre in Vietnam.

In My Lai, a small group of American soldiers from Charlie Company of the Eleventh Brigade, Americal Division, snapped and went on a killing spree, murdering hundreds of unarmed Vietnamese villagers, including women, children and old people. But – and this is important to note – they were finally stopped by other American soldiers.

A US Army scout helicopter pilot, who was flying over the massacre as it was in progress, immediately set his craft down between the marauding soldiers, who were being led by a young lieutenant, and the desperate villagers.

Putting his own life on the line to stop the murders, the pilot, Warrant Officer Hugh Thompson, Junior, saved at least nine villagers who would surely have been killed, arranging to have them evacuated, while the two other members of his chopper crew covered him with drawn weapons. Later, another young American soldier, 22-year-old Ronald Ridenhour, gathered information about the massacre on his own initiative, and at peril to his career, and pushed the government to investigate.

In a similar style, in Iraq, one 24-year-old soldier put his career on the line by reporting to the Army's Criminal Investigations Division about the mistreatment in Abu Ghraib. Specialist Joseph Darby, a military policeman in the same unit with the soldiers charged with the wrongdoing, 'wasn't one that went along with his peers', his small-town high-school football coach told *ABC News*. He was concerned with doing what was right and 'didn't worry about what people thought'.

As Davy Crockett, the American frontiersman in the coonskin cap, said (at least in the '50s Disney Western): 'Be sure you're right, then go ahead.'

In war, when it's kill or be killed, innocents will die and some soldiers will go over the civilised line, but clearly the overall history of Americans in uniform is of trying to do right, and of trying to help the people they've been sent to liberate – whether those people are in Baghdad or Bastogne.

No doubt even now, in Baghdad or Basra, there is some little Iraqi kid chewing American gum and reading American magazines, and becoming enamoured of the future life she imagines herself leading in the United States, just like the British kid who, many years ago in wartime London, was given a stick of gum by an American GI and then went around cleaning up at the soldiers' barracks to make a few pennies, and to obsessively pour over the glossy American magazines of the time. The America-obsessed kid's name? Michael Caine.

Early indications are that the rest of the world agrees that the atrocities in Iraq are aberrations; and that, like Americans themselves, the rest of the world wants the United States to live up to its own best traditions and ideals. That view was epitomised in a recent *New York Times* article, headlined 'War and Abuse Do Little Harm to US Brands', in which a devout Muslim teenager in Singapore, who liked dropping in at his local McDonald's, allowed that not all Americans were bad, just as not all Muslims were.

However, a major study of consumer attitudes in 30 countries, released around the same time as *The New York Times* article, found a worrisome downtrend in the association of the 'concepts of internationalism, equality and other altruistic values' with American culture, according to an *Advertising Age* report, and for the first time since the annual study began in 1998 'respondents' familiarity, claims to use and desire to purchase American products declined'. The countries where there was the least affinity for American culture were Egypt, France, Germany, Italy, Saudi Arabia, Spain, Sweden and Turkey, according to the study, while the countries with the greatest were Australia, Brazil, Hungary, the Philippines, South Africa, Taiwan and Venezuela.

Anti-Americanism may be reflexive in some parts of the globe, especially where people learn about the United States solely from hostile government propaganda, but it's certainly not in others – particularly in those countries whose citizens think it's past time for America to march in and liberate them, too. That, at least, is the gist of a recent essay in the *Chronicle Of Higher Education* by Elinor Burkett, an American journalism teacher, recalling her time abroad as a Fulbright professor in the former Soviet Republic of Kyrgyzstan.

Her suspicious colleagues and students in Kyrgyzstan may have wondered if she was a CIA or FBI agent, but when she travelled to Afghanistan, women kissed her hands and offered thanks for their liberation from the Taliban, she reported. And when she spent time in Myanmar, formerly Burma, where a brutal military dictatorship rules, strangers came up to her and asked why the United States hadn't come to liberate their country the way it had liberated Afghanistan. Ms Burkett, who has written about her adventures in these far-off lands in a book, *So Many Enemies, So Little Time: An American Woman In All The Wrong Places*, also is chairwoman of the department of journalism at the University of Alaska at Fairbanks.

When she finally arrived in Iran, where an epic, if largely covert civic struggle is underway between the forces of Islamic fundamentalism, who control the government, and a nascent student-led civil liberties movement, average, freedom-hungry

Iranians would say to her, 'Why don't more Americans come to Iran?... We love Americans.'

Calls for boycotts of American products continue to fail, even in a hotbed like the Middle East, not only because the big global American corporations purvey products that people everywhere like, but because the same corporations staff their operations locally. So, for example, a McDonald's put out of business anywhere in the Middle East means that a local businessman suffers losses and local citizens become unemployed.

There's also no denying the appeal of America's exuberant, youthful pop culture. Which is not to say that it's not at times crass and in bad taste, appealing shamelessly to sexual and other 'base' urges. It's no accident that the Americans' arrival in Baghdad marked the start of a thriving bar scene in the Green Zone there, and that all kinds of formerly forbidden substances, including Viagra and 'breast enhancement' creams, are suddenly openly available. Back in England, Sloggi, an undergarment company known for its racy, in-your-face, heat-seeking advertising campaigns, put up – near two mosques in Leeds, West Yorkshire – two billboards showing four nearly nude models, with their G-string-clad backsides facing outward. Thongs were the products being touted. Previously, a sexy billboard had gone up in the vicinity of a secondary school. Is this right? Should it be banned? It's shrewd, just as certainly as it's tasteless. But it does suggest a rude question: what are they wearing under those burkas anyway?

Affronted fundamentalists living in the United States and other Western democracies generally have the right to be left alone and not imposed upon, though Americans are unlikely to do away with sexy advertisements any time soon. Fundamentalists also have recourse, in the courts and elsewhere, that they would not themselves grant to 'unbelievers'. In fact, sooner or later, when they come into power, fundamentalist zealots – of whatever stripe – itch for the whip to enforce their beliefs.

Meanwhile, the majority of today's overseas American soldiers themselves, now also armed with DVDs, satellite dishes, MP3 players, CDs and Internet access, will generally continue to be their country's own best cultural salesmen, even in the midst of hostilities and even while punishments are meted out to those who commit atrocities.

Official Hollywood, ever on the lookout for piracy, may not like it, but the truth is that if a movie has been out in a US theatre for a week, 'you can get it here', as one soldier in Iraq said earlier this year. Hip, raucous American pop culture is alive and well throughout the Middle East, as well as in Iraq, where the troops themselves, who have access to everything from *The Simpsons* to *The Sopranos* on satellite or DVD, have taken to greeting each other with, 'Who's your Baghdaddy?'

2 Hollywood And The Great American Myth Machine (Optioning Britain's Best)

First came the movies, then the deluge of television shows. For more than a century, Hollywood's 'product' has entranced generations of kids all around the world, even while some of their elders have fumed. Whether they were kids in Brooklyn or Dublin, Bombay or Hong Kong, they played Hollywood-inspired pretend, ack-acking each other with machine guns, blasting each other with six-shooters or swashbuckling with light sabres. Hollywood created little would-be James Cagneys, Gary Coopers and Harrison Fords everywhere its movies played (and its movies played anywhere there was a pfennig, yuan or a shekel to be made).

In fact, the United States remains, as it has been for decades, the leading exporter of cinema. As far back as the mid-1980s, Jack Valenti, the silver-maned, lantern-jawed president of the Motion Picture Association of America, and Hollywood's highly effective chief lobbyist in Washington (who is expected to retire by the end of 2004), was reporting to the United States Congress that the 'audio-visual sector' had a positive trade balance of $1 billion. That positive entertainment-industry trade balance is now over $5 billion, and growing.

The American entertainment industry taken as a whole, and including everything from films to software, is the second-largest US exporter after aircraft, according to Jeffrey E Garten, the dean of the Yale School of Management, who served as US Commerce Department Under Secretary for International Trade from 1993 to 1995.

More than half of all Hollywood theatrical revenues now come from outside the United States, compared to just 30 per cent in 1980. In the mid-1980s, just over half of the European box office went to American films. By 1990, according to *Screen International*, a trade magazine, American movies accounted for 85 per cent of the box office in Germany, 70 per cent in Italy and 73 per cent in Spain. That same year, at the height of her Material Girl popularity, Madonna's music sales internationally were two-and-a-half times bigger than her sales in the US, according to *Fortune* magazine.

By the mid-1990s, as much as 70 per cent of the film box office in the European Union countries went to American movies, while more than half of Japan's box office was made in the USA. By then, the international box office was big enough to counteract even the biggest domestic film failures in North America. Both *Waterworld*, the bloated science-fiction epic starring Kevin Costner that became a synonym for Hollywood profligacy, and *Judge Dredd*, a comic-book science-fiction film starring Sylvester Stallone, that was judged dreadful by audiences and critics alike, made enough from the international action-and-adventure crowd to overcome American indifference. Perhaps they should have been dubbed for the American market, too.

Almost a decade and a half ago, a young Japanese marketing consultant explained his country's fascination with all things American this way, 'After the war, Japanese youth thought that everything American was cool,' he said, 'because you won [and] American things were best.... When I was nine, my father bought a Sony colour TV, which led to me watching *The Gong Show*. He bought a JVC record player, and I listened to Jimi Hendrix and Santana.'

By then, the Japanese were beginning their $12 billion investment spree in American media companies, aware that the Hollywood-centric media business was a growth industry. Of course, a Hollywood studio is a factory where the assets march out the front gates every night, as a wag once said. Partly in recognition of that fact, and partly to distinguish it from the smoke-belching factories of an earlier era that produced manufactured goods, the Japanese began to call the media industry *omizu shobai*, or the 'water business'.

Today, the fascination with American pop culture has simply grown exponentially. It means that hip Japanese kids dress (and listen to) American hip-hop. It means they still flock to American movies – for example, *The Lord Of The Rings: Return Of The King*, the third film in the trilogy, which was the Number One film at the box office for nine of the first ten weeks it played in Japan.

Break-dancing American B-boys and other multiculturally inclined hipsters return the favour by being enamoured of Japanese samurai movies and Japanese manga and anime, as their comic books and cartoons are called. In fact, in 2002, Japan, which creates some 60 per cent of the cartoons aired on televisions around the world, exported animated products to the United States worth approximately $4,360,000,000, according to the Japan External Trade Organisation.

Traditional Japanese anime companies are looking to expand in the US beyond their current hip-hop, sci-fi, teenage-boy base, so in their latest anime films they have begun incorporating the Pixar-like, computer-generated animation style that has been such a hit in American animated pictures from *Toy Story* to *Finding Nemo*.

As novelist Frederic Raphael once put it, Hollywood has 'proved a more reliable, cost-effective means of securing world domination than any nuclear arsenal or diplomatic démarche'. That's right, Fred, but it's only true because folks everywhere know that Hollywood puts on a pretty good show.

All around the world everyone knows the Hollywood sign, rising imperially above the LA smog at the top of the Hollywood hillside that cups quiet Beechwood Canyon, just east of the constant hum of traffic zipping through the Cahuenga Pass. It is the symbol of the triumphant Hollywood film business. But contrary to conventional wisdom, the American film business wasn't born in sunny, hazy Los Angeles. Commercial American movies began on the other side of the country, almost two decades before the first cry of 'Action!' ever echoed in Hollywood. The first American movies – jerky, flickering silent shorts featuring scantily clad dancing girls or preening muscle men – mesmerised early viewers in the 1890s in New York City. They were exhibited in arcades mostly, in the 'kinetoscope', a device invented by Thomas Edison, America's most famous inventor. These proto-movies often were made in West Orange, New Jersey, where the prolific Edison had constructed his 'Black Maria', a black tar-paper-covered building on a pivot that could be turned along the arc of the sunlight coming in from a window above. Soon, the early kinetoscopes, which enabled individuals to watch moving pictures, through peepholes, were replaced by movies projected on screens in front of whole audiences, in 'nickelodeons', parlours and theatres.

In those early days of the medium, making a movie required natural light, and that eventually sent filmmakers West, in search of year-around sunshine.

Edison, the prolific inventor, who jealously guarded his copyrights and patents, may have had a hand, too, in the westward migration of the East Coast motion-picture entrepreneurs, especially in the years immediately after 1909 when he and a few other movie producers formed the Motion Picture Patents Company. This was partly intended to protect Edison's patents of early filmmaking equipment and partly to stop the proliferating independent 'interlopers' in what Edison regarded as his business.

At any rate, Arizona was the intended destination that would have been the nascent film industry's new home, or so the oft-told story goes...

In 1914, aspiring filmmakers Cecil B DeMille and Samuel Goldwyn, intent on finding a suitable location to film *The Squaw Man*, their latest project, headed west to Flagstaff, Arizona, in search of 'alkaline flats and purple sage'. But when they stepped off the train, they found 'snow, not...mesas and cacti but...white-capped mountains and near-alpine vistas', according to an account in the *Tucson Weekly*. And so, instead of setting up to make their movie regardless, or travelling farther south, to Tucson, where they would have found exactly what they were looking for, they got right back on the train and continued on to its last stop, a dusty, rambunctious western town whose population was about to explode. That town was Los Angeles.

At the close of the 19th century, the City of Angels, which had been incorporated 50 years before, was still merely a parched desert town, known best for its orange groves. In those years, cosmopolitan San Francisco was the premiere California city, and LA was merely an out-of-the-way afterthought, clinging in the hazy basin between the desert and the sea.

By 1900, thanks to the discovery of oil in the area a few years before, LA's population had finally topped the 100,000 mark. By 1913, the little city had finally solved its perpetual water supply with an aqueduct, built by William Mulholland, that brought pure water from the Owens Valley, some 370km (230 miles) to the north, in the form of snow melt from the Sierra mountains. The machinations and the land speculation surrounding the construction of that aqueduct eventually were fictionalised in the classic film-noir movie, *Chinatown*.

In 1914, the same year DeMille and Goldwyn arrived, the Panama Canal opened, and suddenly little Los Angeles was 12,875km (8,000 miles) closer by sea to New York and the big cities of the East Coast. The boom was underway and within six short years, the population of the City of Angels stood at one million.

When he stepped off the train at the end of that fateful journey in 1914, Cecil B DeMille promptly rented a yellow barn in the middle of a Hollywood orange grove and converted it into the city's first studio.

DW Griffith had made *In Old California*, a well-received movie, in the area a few years before. But while Griffith's movie was the exception for the New York-dominated film industry, DeMille's *The Squaw Man* became the first example of the New Rule.

Squaw Man, which cost around $45,000 to make, earned more than $250,000 at the box office. The movies had found their new home.

The United States domination of the international film industry is nothing new. It has been true since before the movies learned to talk. Some of the movie-influenced kids outside the United States grew up to be filmmakers themselves, and in the process tough-guy Humphrey Bogart in *The Maltese Falcon* morphed into louche Jean-Paul Belmondo in the influential French New Wave noir *Breathless*, who in turn was reincarnated as Richard Gere, in the inevitable American remake.

Think about it: the great Hollywood film director of the sumptuous, American-produced film version of Jane Austen's *Sense And Sensibility*, that quintessential story of 18th-century English society, is Ang Lee, a Taiwanese.

The makers of popular culture have always been its first, and most complete, victims, as the philosopher once said. So it is no accident that in recent times California, the Golden State with an economy larger than most countries and which is the home to Hollywood, has been governed by two actual movie stars, one of whom wasn't even born in the United States and presents himself as the personification of the American immigrant dream.

America has always proffered itself as one of the only lands on earth where an under-educated immigrant with an accent might better himself through diligence and hard work, might rise to the highest levels of society, might even become one day, say, a movie star or perhaps the governor of a great state.

Or both.

His goals in life, said Arnold Schwarzenegger's friends from his youth in Austria, were to move to America, become a famous actor and marry a Kennedy.

But movie stardom and marriage to a Kennedy turned out to be only the first act of the one-time Austrian bodybuilder's American Dream. In 2003 the action hero announced on a late-night television talk show that he was running for Governor of California, in a recall election.

Like the late Ronald Reagan, another movie star turned politician, Arnold Schwarzenegger seemed to be made of Teflon, at least as far as the voters were concerned. On 7 October 2003, the California electorate shrugged off accusations from at least a dozen women, who claimed the action-movie star had groped them, and elected him governor of America's Golden State.

It's hard to say if Arnold Schwarzenegger is more unlikely as a movie star or as a popular and successful politician (and he has been so successful that what was once a movie joke is now an actual possibility: changing the Constitution so that a 'naturalised' citizen like Schwarzenegger can run for president). He's also a Republican married to the daughter of the Democratic party's royal family.

It is at once so utterly implausible and so typically an all-American rise from humble roots and despite formidable obstacles that it might be the plot of a Frank Capra movie.

It is no accident that other countries, particularly France and China, fear domination by the images and sounds of American popular culture – Americanisation in the guise of globalisation, as the opponents of America's pop culture put it. That fear has led to what the United States regards as 'cultural protectionism', and the French and Chinese, among others, regard as exercising their 'cultural sovereignty'; namely, the restrictions and quotas that other countries put on America's television, music and films.

France, for example, mandates that 40 per cent of all television programming and all music played on TV or the radio must be French, while Canada, America's neighbour to the North, requires that 60 per cent of broadcast-television programming be of domestic vintage, as well as 35 per cent of the music played on the radio during prime time.

In 2003, China allowed just 20 foreign movies to be shown in the vast country's theatres. Still, according to *Asia Pacific Arts*, a publication of the UCLA Asia Institute, among the most popular movies in China that year were *Pirates Of The Caribbean*, *The Italian Job* and *The Matrix: Revolutions*.

But quotas on American cultural exports are nothing new either. As far back as the 1920s, well before the advent of the 'talkies', Germany was limiting the number of American movies that could be imported and shown.

Today, it's more than just movies and other entertainment that are marked 'Made in America', and that fact makes other governments and their elites react with predictable disapproval. Time Warner's Cable News Network, for example, is ubiquitous throughout the world, reaching approximately 200 million households in more than 200 countries. CNN's main American cable-news competitor is the Fox News Channel, a part of Rupert Murdoch's News Corporation, the international, vertically integrated media empire that also owns: the Twentieth Century Fox film and television studio; the Fox Broadcasting Company; the Fox Television Stations; the BskyB, Sky Italia and DirecTV satellite operations; *The Sun* and *The Times* in the United Kingdom; the *New York Post* in the United States and many, many other newspaper, TV, publishing and other assets, including a television network in the southern Chinese province of Guandong.

Like Mister Schwarzenegger before him, Mister Murdoch, an Australian by birth, became an American citizen – in the latter case to fulfil the requirement that only American citizens can own an American television network, although his company continued to be based in Australia. But by 2004, 75 per cent of News Corporation's revenues and profits were being generated in the United States, so the corporation itself was reincorporated in America, becoming at last a US-based company.

But even as one media baron and his empire were immigrating to America, American culture was heading out in the other direction, crossing every other frontier.

'Images of America are so pervasive in this global village that it is almost as if instead of the world immigrating to America, America has emigrated to the world, allowing people to aspire to be Americans even in distant countries,' as former Canadian Prime Minister Kim Campbell once put it.

Not surprisingly, America's movie, TV and music moguls are avid free-traders – not surprising, given that just last year a congressman from California, home state to not only Hollywood, but the high-tech businesses of Silicon Valley and the vast San Fernando Valley-based hard-core pornography industry, estimated that 'entertainment and other intellectual property products, from works of literature to computer software', annually generate $500 billion in worldwide sales.

America seems secure – for now – as the sole pop-cultural superpower, and there are no particular barriers to artists, entertainers and cultural products going from the rest of the world back to the USA. Quite the opposite, in fact.

Even as American blockbuster pictures continue to dominate internationally, the stream of foreign films onto US screens has continued to increase, year after year.

In television, more than at any time in the medium's history, Over There is where you go to find your next televised sensation. And the many new start-up cable networks in the United States, which are jockeying for carriage on digital cable and satellite, in a spectrum 'land rush' unmatched since the early days of cable itself, often go abroad for inexpensive and promotable programming.

Consider, for example, one such new network, Reality TV, that ballyhooed the premiere of five new shows, all from other English-speaking countries. The shows on which Reality TV is pinning its future are *Taking It Off*, from Canada, which follows a group of people as they try to lose weight; *Dream Factory*, from Australia, which tracks a group of young hopefuls trying to become stars in Hollywood; *Lad's Army*, from England, which follows a group of young men as they endure rigorous British military training; *Girl Cops*, also from England, which follows a group of, well, girl cops; and *Hospital*, from New Zealand, which follows a group of doctors, nurses and patients in a major hospital.

The lesson of all these reality shows? To get ahead in today's TV world, it's good to be from an English-speaking country.

The same is true of film. When you venture into the great American multiplex for a movie today, odds are that the latest international blockbuster will star or be directed by a Brit, an Aussie or a New Zealander, or it might be derived from a British novel or series of novels – take, for recent example, *Master And Commander*, *The Lord Of The Rings* trilogy or the *Harry Potter* films. If you turn on the tube, the big reality/game hits of the day, from *Survivor* to *Fear Factor*, are likely to be based on Brit or Aussie formats, too.

Consider this, however, is there anything more American than taking the best of other countries and cultures and selling it back to their people?

Naturally, American television executives are quite pleased to 'give back' too. No doubt in that spirit, the makers of *America's Next Top Model*, the biggest hit ever on UPN (the United Paramount Network, the smallest of the six American broadcast networks, which is a part of the Viacom media conglomerate and also includes MTV and CBS), have now sold the show in more than 40 different countries, including territories in Europe, Asia and Latin America. They have also sold the 'format' in even more parts of the globe, including in Russia, where, according to the showbusiness trade papers, *Top Model* is already a hit.

Over at ABC, the network owned by The Walt Disney Company, its plastic-surgery-plus series, *Extreme Makeover*, has been sold in more than 120 different territories, from Belgium to Hong Kong and New Zealand. Almost everywhere it airs, the show, in which contestants get the Cinderella treatment via the services of not only plastic surgeons but cosmetic dental specialists, make-up artists and personal trainers, has been a hit with the young audiences that advertisers around the world lust after.

In this new millennium, after the American Century, there may finally be a competitor for pop-cultural pre-eminence on the horizon. Already, globalisation is a fact of corporate life on the big Hollywood studio lots. One studio, Columbia, is owned by Sony, a Japanese electronics manufacturer. As we know, another, Twentieth Century Fox, is owned by News Corporation, the international vertically integrated media company that until mid-2004 was based in Australia and is headed by Rupert Murdoch. Yet another studio, Universal, in recent years went from being owned by a Japanese company, Matsushita, to ownership by a French company, Vivendi, which went nearly bankrupt in its efforts to transform itself from a Gallic utility company to an international media conglomerate recognised on the Hollywood stage. (Historically, 'foreigners' haven't done very well in their attempts to become Hollywood players: Credit Lyonnais, the French state-owned bank, went from disaster to disaster when it began to loan money to Hollywood companies in the 1990s.) Universal's ownership passed from Vivendi to General Electric, the diversified American conglomerate that also owns the National Broadcasting Network (NBC), which in turn recently acquired Telemundo, the number two Spanish-language broadcaster in the United States. All of these studios, and The Walt Disney Company, among others, also are busily proliferating television channels throughout the world. The name of that game, as it is for Coke and McDonald's, is extending the brand.

Of course, it's never been easy to play the pop culture game Hollywood style, and it's never been pricier than right now. In his valedictory address to Hollywood theatrical exhibitors, at the annual Las Vegas gala-cum-convention called ShoWest in spring of 2004, retiring Motion Picture Association (MPAA) President Jack Valenti detailed the astronomical costs to play in the same game as the Seven Hollywood Sisters of the MPAA.

Simple production costs by the MPAA studio members in 2003 were up to a staggering average of $63,800,000 per movie, while average per-picture marketing expenditures added another $39 million, for the almost unbelievable total of $102,900,000 – the average cost to make and market a major American studio movie in 2003.

In a nod to the crucial importance to the industry of box office receipts from outside the United States, Mister Valenti's last state-of-the-industry report was also his first to break down international revenues as well. In 2003, international box office, including Canada, brought in $10,855,000,000, or 53 per cent of the worldwide $20 billion total.

Just over half, 51 per cent, of that international total came from Europe, 35 per cent came from the Asia-Pacific region, 7 per cent came from Latin America and 6 per cent from

Canada. All of those areas, with the possible exception of Canada and a few western European countries, are considered 'evolving' markets, with demand, like population and gross national product, soaring.

In Russia, for example, in 1999, the year after the dissolution of the Soviet Union, American movies made just $18 million at the box office, in a country with around 145 million people, three-quarters of whom lived in its major cities. In 2003, by comparison, the Russian box-office total was $190 million. And it is expected to rise. Part of the reason for that increase is a proliferation of movie screens; in St Petersburg, for example, in 2004 alone, the number of movie screens is expected to jump from 28 to 90 by year's end. According to an English-language St. Petersburg newspaper, 80 per cent of the audience for those screens has not been going to movies at all in recent years, but is expected to be attracted by the opportunity to see 'Hollywood blockbusters' locally.

In 2003, in fact, seven major-studio Hollywood movies each brought in more than $250 million from non-US markets. Among them was one animated picture, the charming Pixar-animated *Finding Nemo*.

That's entertainment. Or as the oratorically inclined Mr Valenti put it to a gathering of financial analysts a year earlier, 'The future of movie entertainment springs from the human condition's grand simplicity.

'It is this,' he continued. 'People, no matter their culture, creed or country, want to be entertained [and] that human desire has never shrunk or faltered in over 2,500 years. The human hankering to enjoy entertainment remains undiminished to this very hour.'

True enough, Mister Valenti. And the English language is still, by far, the dominant *lingua franca* of international entertainment and popular culture, but can that dominance last in a changing world beset by uncertainties, new dangers and opportunities? Perhaps, eventually, the pop culture of the 21st century will be dominated by China or India, two vast, rapidly evolving markets that have, in the presidential political year of 2004, become domestic political targets of easy resort in the United States. After all, Indians, despite Hindi and the 32 other languages that are spoken by at least one million persons, also speak English, which, thanks to the good offices of the British Empire, remains the language of upward mobility – the language of the professionals, the upper classes and the elites. And at least since the days of Archie Leach, and right up to Russell Crowe and Colin Farrell, an accent that hints of the Empire does quite well in Anglophone Hollywood, too. Just ask Michael Caine.

But, just as 'France' has become a shorthand for anti-Americanism of all sorts, but particularly in foreign policy, and 'China' has come to mean cheap goods manufactured under dubious auspices that are pouring into the United States, 'India' has come to stand for cheap, English-speaking labour and the 'out-sourcing' of scarce white-collar and increasingly high-technology American jobs.

The yard (garage) sale is one quintessentially American phenomenon that has morphed into big business on the Internet in the form of eBay. And eBay, ever on the lookout for expansion, is eyeing Chinese speakers in China, Hong Kong, Singapore and Taiwan. The reason? Within the next decade or so, China is expected to become eBay's second largest market.

But the gathering challenge to American cultural hegemony from Asia doesn't end there. Consider this: in a 1999 BBC online poll asking who was the millennium's biggest star, the winner was none other than...

Ambitabh Bachchan.

The Big B, as he's called, is a major movie star, Hasselhoff handsome, with tens of millions of avid fans, from the subcontinent to the Middle East to London and New York.

But he's a creation of Bollywood, the Indian film industry based in Mumbai (as Bombay, the largest city in India, is now known), not Hollywood.

Hollywood may make unmatched billions in international revenue every year, but it's Bollywood, not Hollywood, that actually has the bigger film industry and makes the most movies, around 900 annually, which is more than three times what Hollywood turns out. Television arrived in India at the end of the 1950s, and it wasn't long before the country was enthralled by its home-grown televised soap operas. And the Indian television marketplace, with more than 100 satellite-delivered channels, is today the third largest in the world.

For most of its history, 'Bollywood' (a term that combines 'Bombay' and 'Hollywood') has been a synonym for florid, over-the-top melodramas and musicals with big, glitzy dance numbers that Busby Berkeley might have admired. A typical story goes something like this: poor boy loves rich girl, overcomes parental disapproval, as well as many other obstacles, before finally marriage ensues. And of course, everyone, including the in-laws, lives happily ever after.

But the more traditional, simplistic and insular formulas of Bollywood are being transformed by the demands of evermore sophisticated audiences, particularly in the Indian diaspora, who vote with their Indian rupees, their British pounds and their American dollars. Already, for example, the United Kingdom and the United States, both of which are home to large South Asian minorities, account for some 55 per cent of Indian film-industry ticket sales outside of India.

It's a familiar story, whether the immigrant home is of Indian, Mexican or Russian heritage: the older generation likes the old ways just fine, but the kids, bopping around the streets of London or New York, they're another story altogether, and demographically speaking, sooner or later they get the say.

That generational sea change is one reason why 2002 was such an out-and-out disaster at the Bollywood box office. The big Hindi-language segment of the Indian film industry actually lost money that year – $62.5 million, to be exact. The reason: the tired, recycled formulas of the Hindi-language filmmakers themselves. 'How long can you keep giving them stale stuff churned out from really bad stories?' is how one producer put it.

And so, not surprisingly, in 2003 the biggest picture at the Bollywood box office broke away from the old formulas, and it was a hit with US and UK South Asians, too. *Koi... Mil Gaya* ('I've Found Someone'), the big winner at the Indian box office, was – of all things – a science-fiction movie about a 'mentally challenged' boy who makes contact with an alien. Reviewers noted that the nearly three-hour-long picture blithely bent genres and mixed plots from famous sci-fi films, from *ET* to *Charly*. It was the first science-fiction flick ever made in the Hindi language and, naturally, it also included a romance and several song-and-dance musical numbers.

By best estimates, more than half a million South Asians live in the tri-state New York City area, which includes the suburbs of New Jersey and Connecticut. Many more than that live in the Greater London area. It's precisely those population concentrations that have inspired theatrical producers in both cities to bring a Bollywood musical melodrama to the legitimate stage, in a lavish $14 million production called *Bombay Dreams* that is just finishing a two-year run in London, where it was produced by composer Andrew Lloyd Webber, and is set to debut on Broadway. The show, an extravagant musical about – of course – the rise of a poor untouchable to movie stardom, includes kitschy Bollywood-style production numbers and romantic tunes by AR Rahman, the most popular Indian film composer of the time.

Of course, multinationals like Sony and News Corporation, owners of big American Hollywood studios, haven't ignored the subcontinent either, and they are beginning to pay attention to the South Asian diasporas, too. It has not escaped the notice of the big media conglomerates that India, with over one billion citizens – who altogether speak more than a hundred distinct languages – is the world's largest democracy and that its economy is the world's fourth largest, and growing rapidly. (But the Indian economy is not growing nearly fast enough or big enough for the estimated 300 million, mostly rural and lower-caste Indians who still live on less than one dollar per day, and that's why the ruling government of the Hindu-nationalist Bharatiya Janata Party – which took credit for the heavily hyped, high-tech-based surge in the country's economy in the past few years – was voted out of office in an upset in the May 2004 national election. Its victorious opposition, the Indian National Congress Party, won by promising to spread the economic benefits more widely across Indian society, beyond the Bangalore-based technocrats of the emerging middle class.)

In India, the multinational media companies of Hollywood are starting up their own Hindi-speaking networks and satellite operations, carrying everything from blockbuster Bollywood musicals to Hindi-pop music videos. Meanwhile, in yet another example of the two-way pop cultural traffic, traditional Bollywood players have begun making more English-language pictures and tailoring their products for the more westernised tastes of the Indian diaspora in Britain and America.

Of course Hollywood even tried its own version of the Bollywood comedy with music. *The Guru*, a 2002 film starring Heather Graham, Marisa Tomei and Jimi Mistry, tells the charming story of a handsome and innocent Indian dance teacher (Mistry), who knows all the words of all John Travolta music from *Grease* and *Saturday Night Fever*. Of course, the young man comes to New York convinced he will become a star, but finds himself acting in a porno film instead and falling in love with his engaged-to-be-married lead porno actress

(Graham). At the same time, a young socialite (Tomei) becomes his wide-eyed acolyte, believing him to be the Guru of Sex. One complication leads to another, and soon Misty has become a media sensation. The marriage, the happy ending and the final musical fantasy number are straight out of Bollywood's sensibility. The movie was small and didn't make a big splash, but it did make a profit, and ultimately that was what counted.

On American television, too, the Indian diaspora is on the verge of one of the ultimate pop culture accolades: a television series that revolves around it and its humorous foibles. 'Unlikely', 'blended' families are a situation comedy staple, whether that family includes gay in-laws, White children living with a Black family (or vice versa) or a wise-cracking alien living in the house. American TV's latest unlikely family will be found in *Never Mind Nirvana*, a potential NBC series, that intends to mine the comic possibilities that arise when an Indian-American doctor's immigrant parents move in with him and his Caucasian wife. One of the show's executive producers is David Schwimmer, 'Ross' of *Friends* fame. Despite that connection, at the time of this writing, whether or not the show will be picked up by the network for the new season is still unknown.

What is known is that, in another example of today's two-way TV-show traffic, American audiences will soon be watching (on BBC America) *The Kumars at No. 42*, the hit U.K. comedy about a North London Indian family that hosts a talk show in its backyard.

In America, News Corporation's Fox Broadcasting may be known for its outrageous reality-programming stunts. In the UK, *The Sun* newspaper is known for its Page Three girls. But India is still a country where a movie with lesbian scenes can draw outraged crowds of Hindus protesting outside the theatre, and Mister Murdoch did not become fabulously wealthy by misconstruing his audiences. So when News Corp's Star World, its Indian programming service, took the reality concept to the subcontinent, the result was tailored to Indian sensibilities. What Star came up with was not *American Idol* or an extreme makeover show, but *India Child Genius*, a talent show looking to crown India's smartest 10–13-year-old kid.

Meanwhile, back in the United States, a group of influential advertising and marketing executives formed a group called Business For Diplomatic Action to combat a declining 'regard' for all things American in the wider world. Yes, one their first actions was to fund yet another study, and yes, the new executive director of the new group was a former colleague of Charlotte Beers, whose efforts as Under Secretary for Public Diplomacy and Public Affairs were widely regarded as futile and misguided.

The new executive director, Cari Eggspuehler, said the group would encourage American media companies to be more sensitive to how their cultural exports played on the world stage; in other words, she said, they would avoid *Baywatch*-like stereotypes.

Now wait a minute, Ms Eggspuehler! Why so dismissive of *Baywatch*'s vanguard role in the overthrow of Soviet Communism? Don't you remember David Hasselhoff at the barricade between East and West, singing his heart out?

At least one media company has already risen to the challenge to replace jiggle with uplift, coming up with a pilot for a proposed reality series that would focus on young Americans working for foreign companies and dealing with foreign cultures, while also showing young foreigners working for American companies and dealing with the 'foreignness' of American culture.

Even though she obviously doesn't 'get' what *Baywatch* is selling, the general kind of cultural sensitivity and cultural give-and-take that the new executive director of Business For Diplomatic Action has called for is squarely in the American tradition, too. So are the mixed-race, mixed-culture kids that can be found on the streets of any big American city, or on the streets of London or Paris for that matter, and who are an utterly welcome alternative to the benighted days of anti-miscegenation. So, for that matter, is the phenomenon of big corporations discovering previously ignored immigrant diasporas and previously ignored foreign markets, and previously ignored urban demographic groups, all in the interest of making a buck.

Doing well by doing good. Now, doesn't that sound just like the classic American Way at its best?

3 Seattle: Microsoft And Starbucks – Code And Coffee Conquer The World

Walk over to the next corner in most any big city in the Western world, and it's déjà vu all over again – the green emblem, the rich aroma, the knots of earnest hipster kids lounging and sipping, book bags thrown over the backs of chairs. And what's in those book bags? Yes, of course, notebook and laptop computers running Microsoft's ubiquitous code.

Seattle is the home of two quintessentially American success stories, Starbucks and Microsoft. One represents the triumph of the simple good idea, obvious in retrospect – sell fancy coffee at $3 (£2) a cup! The other represents a marketing and strategic triumph, the victory of what is arguably merely the second-best idea, though it is defended by a phalanx of the best lawyers and propelled forward by a first-rate marketing scheme; after all, Apple's operating system, it's generally recognised, is superior to Microsoft's Windows. How did it happen and why were these worldwide influences born in America's Pacific Northwest?

Seattle also gave birth to grunge, arguably the most influential pop music of the late 1980s and early 1990s, which, right at its influential apogee, became the soundtrack to a cautionary tale about the mortal dangers of the rock 'n' roll life – a cautionary tale of operatic, even epic, proportions.

That coffee, those laptops, the music? Smells like teen spirit.

Seattle in the State of Washington is a lovely, liveable jewel of a port city – rightly called the Emerald City – situated on Elliott Bay, a part of Puget Sound, some 200km (125 miles) from the open waters of the Pacific Ocean. The city is a gateway to the spectacular vistas of Alaska, and was the jumping off point for the fortune hunters of the Klondike and the Alaskan Gold Rush, and it is also continental America's closest port to the distant ports of call of the Far East, a full 1,600km (995 miles) closer than the port of San Francisco.

Seattle lies in a picturesque corner of America, in a geography of unsurpassed natural beauty, encompassing not only water but snow-covered mountains and deep green forests. The city, named for a chief of one of the local Indian tribes, was founded a century and a half ago by loggers, fishermen and seafarers, railroad men and miners. Summers are generally cool there and winters are generally mild.

If you're looking for a reason to love America, gather up your umbrella and raincoat, pop over to Seattle and have a look around. Talk to the locals, who run the gamut from Scandinavians to Asians, and are generally cosmopolitan, friendly and unaffected. They're industrious, too. Perhaps it's the coffee.

The first Starbucks, a coffee shop named after the hardy chief mate in Herman Melville's 1851 masterpiece, *Moby Dick*, opened in 1971 in Seattle's Pike Place Market near the glittering waterfront. Melville's whaling epic was published the same year that Seattle was founded, and its collection of colourful seamen might well have dropped anchor there and come ashore for a cup. Starbuck, the chief mate and the voice of reason and prudence aboard mad Captain Ahab's *Pequod*, loved his coffee, Starbucks the coffee purveyor maintains, though there appears to be scant evidence for it in Mister Melville's mighty text.

For the first dozen or so years of the coffee shop's existence, it sold coffee beans over the counter and nothing much happened that would suggest Starbuck's Coffee Company would ever become a world-girdling whale of a corporation. Then, in the mid-1980s, something wonderfully unexpected happened: Starbucks tried out its 'coffee-bar' concept at a new location in downtown Seattle. The original owners were dubious but, like the brew itself, that simple concept turned out to be an eye opener.

Many modern American commercial success stories depend on the over-arching vision of one hard-charging executive, and in this instance that visionary came from faraway Canarsie, in Brooklyn. Howard Schultz came West and joined the company as its marketing director in 1982, when it consisted of just four stores that sold beans, not drinks. He rose to become its chief executive officer, then its chief strategist. And it was the estimable Mister Schultz who was responsible for the coffee bar's downtown tryout.

Like many another empire builder, Mr Schultz, who rose from poverty, didn't simply have a plan – open a store every day, provide stock options and health-care plans, even for part-time workers, because ultimately it's a savings, cutting down employee turnover – he also had a philosophy. In a demitasse cup it was: don't be threatened by people smarter than you, seek to renew yourself even when you are hitting home runs and between home and work exists a third place and that's what Starbucks has to become!

In his vision, the lowly coffee bean partook in an almost religious mystery. Drinking coffee is a ritual, filled with 'mystery and romance', he said, and a Starbucks coffee house is at the same time both a home away from home and a temple that is both an expression of that ritual and of an entire culture built around that incomparable sip of coffee.

By the end of the 1980s, the company was growing rapidly, from 17 locations in 1987 (including the first Chicago Starbucks), to 55 just two years later. Back then, there were other purveyors of fancy coffee drinks in quaint little shops, the trendy little Coffee Bean chain in Los Angeles being one example, but only Starbucks kept growing and growing. By the time the first Starbucks opened in Los Angeles, just two years after that, there were 116 locations. The 1990s was the decade of the company's most explosive growth: 272 stores by the end of 1993; 425, including the first in New York, a year later.

By the time Londoners were sipping their first tall lattes in 1998, there were almost 1,900 Starbucks locations, and a year after that the first Starbucks opened its doors in China. At the turn of the millennium, Starbucks had grown to more than 3,500 coffee houses. And in 2001, 30 years after its founding, the smell of its coffee could finally be found wafting along the cobblestone streets of the Continent, beginning with a Starbucks in Zurich.

Today, there are more than 7,500 Starbucks locations, in North and South America; in Europe, from Switzerland to France and even Italy, home of the homemade cappuccino; in the Middle East, from Oman to Turkey, where for centuries they've loved their tiny cups of strong, muddy coffee, and throughout Asia, in China, Korea, Indonesia and Japan, where tea drinking has long been elevated to ceremony. Naturally, Starbucks now owns, among its other assets, a tea company, too.

Some 25 million people a week stop in to a Starbucks. But not everyone is happy living in a world dominated by the Seattle-based coffee company that expects to add 1,300 more coffee houses to its empire in 2004 and eventually to expand to 25,000 stores. It's actually become something of joke to complain about Starbucks, and those small, readily recognisable and usually street-level shops with big tinted picture windows make a ready target for anti-globalisation protesters.

Rocks are one thing, jokes are another. 'D'Oh!' as Homer Simpson would say. One mark of most made-in-America popular culture is that it regards absolutely everything as fair game, and that means that everything is a potential satirical target. So, naturally there came an episode of the ever-droll animated *Simpsons*, in which Bart found himself in a shopping mall that contained – aye caramba! – almost nothing but

Starbucks (the one store that wasn't a Starbucks already was on the verge of turning into one). In *The Spy Who Shagged Me*, the second entry in the big-screen *James Bond* spoof series starring Mike Myers as 'Austin Powers', the snaggle-toothed Carnaby Street-suited spy, it is none other than a Starbucks that turns out to be the headquarters lair for his nemesis, Doctor Evil. And when, in spring 2004, a US government agency released a report critical of the amount of caffeine in children's diets, a late-night TV comic extolled the new line of Gerber baby food, featuring vanilla latte. It was of course, he said, from Starbucks.

Like McDonald's, that other great symbol of American ubiquity, part of what Starbucks is selling – whether it's in Anaheim, California or Zurich, Switzerland – is utter reliability and an absolute certainty that the coffee will taste the same everywhere, perhaps not as great as the local brew in the other little coffee shop down the street, but the same as in every other Starbucks; that the ambience will be the same, right down to those couches and the music, also for sale, in every single Starbucks coffee house; that the bathrooms will be reasonably clean and that the employees will deliver the same professional level of service, partly because they're invested in the company's success, too.

One of the great Starbucks insights of its early days was that the people who patronised coffee shops, and paid premium prices for premium coffee, were sometimes intimidated by the uber-cool, don't-bother-me-I'm-busy attitude of underpaid employees at other coffee shops, who, whether they were in LA or not, often seemed to project the insufferably superior attitude of aspiring actors and would-be directors, momentarily slumming.

Starbucks employees may be as poorly paid as any other service-industry workers, but they have the stock options, the health plans and the rigorous training to inspire them to do better.

Interestingly enough, 'doing better' isn't exactly the image projected by the other world-girdling Seattle-based company, located just across town. 'Tougher' – that's the word Microsoft's many competitors have always said best applies.

It's irresistibly tempting to imagine a pair of geeky young men, a gawky Harvard dropout and his long-time pal, strolling the Seattle waterfront sometime in the late 1970s or early '80s and stopping in at one of the original Starbucks for beans to brew up some nice hot drinks while they talk obsessively about Microsoft, the company they've just formed.

Maybe earlier, in 1974, it was over coffee that Bill Gates and Paul Allen, the future young founders of Microsoft, got the brainstorm to 'cold call' the manufacturers of the Altair 8080, the first micro-computer intended for the then-nonexistent home market, and tell them that they had designed software for the new machine.

Of course, it wasn't true, but the fib got them a meeting and young Paul and boyish Bill pulled all-nighters writing computer code. Seriously – could they have done it without the lowly coffee bean?

By the time, in 1984, that Howard Schultz convinced the original owners to test out his transforming vision of the Starbucks coffee bar, young Bill Gates might well have been aware of it. After all his father, Bill Gates Senior, who was a partner in Seattle's biggest law firm, Preston Gates, represented Schultz when the transplanted New Yorker took Starbucks over from its founding partners (who'd resisted his plans for expansion), a year later.

'A lawyer's eyes start to sparkle when he sees a person like Howard come in with a plan like Starbucks,' the senior Gates recently told *Fortune* magazine. 'Howard has an ability that isn't widespread. He is very directed and dogged, and a very decent person too.'

So from the earliest days of both companies there was at least that lawyerly connection. It's not so hard to imagine that there was more.

Maybe when, in 1981, Gates and Allen sold their MS-DOS operating system to Big Blue – IBM – it wasn't simply the fact that the guy with the better operating system happened to be out of the office the day that IBM's representatives came to call, and in his absence no one would sign the non-disclosure agreement Big Blue required, as the famous story goes. Maybe the Microsoft upstarts got their edge from the stimulation to be had courtesy of Starbucks. Or maybe it was the other guy who was out for a delicious cup of coffee. At any rate, Microsoft had the smarts (and the cash) to buy out another early Seattle-created operating system, and that became the basis of MS-DOS.

The same may have been true when they announced in 1983 that they were in development for a graphical user interface (GUI) called Windows for their MS-DOS code. It was of course based on, and reverse-engineered from, Apple's existing interface for its Macintosh computer, running on its own operating code. And that presented issues that ended up in the hands of lawyers. In fact, Bill Gates, the clever son of the prominent lawyer, created a company that deployed phalanxes of lawyers like myrmidons to fend off and overcome competitors and would-be regulators all along its historic march to worldwide ubiquity.

There was litigation and threatened litigation, practically from the earliest days of Microsoft history. For example, the earliest version of Windows couldn't use a trash can or overlapping windows, because they were (arguably) proprietary features of the Apple GUI. It wasn't until after Microsoft reached a licensing agreement with Apple, perhaps over several cups of Starbucks, that later Windows iterations were able to incorporate the features.

There is a saying famous among cynical American journalists: freedom of the press is for those who own one. Perhaps then, a key to understanding Microsoft's success – beyond the unparalleled importance of being in the right place at the right time, and beyond its undoubted marketing acumen – is a similar insight: justice in the American civil justice system is for those who have hired the best lawyers. And in Seattle, there was no better lawyer – or legal advisor – than the man who raised young Bill Gates.

Bill Gates, born in 1955 and raised in upper-middle-class comfort in Seattle, was introduced to his first computer at Lakeside Prep School in 1968, and by all accounts it was love at first sight. In fact, Bill and his pal Paul, who would go on to found Microsoft together, promptly taught themselves how to hack the school's donated computers. According to legend, when they crashed the system, they were discovered, but instead of being punished were hired by the computer company itself, which paid them in computer time.

From the start, young Bill was a geek deluxe, spending all his free time, and a considerable amount of class time, learning how to use and program the new machines.

By autumn of 1973 Bill Gates was off to Harvard, and he spent most of his time in the computer centre there, too. A year later came the fateful Altair 8080 cold call, and a year after that Gates had dropped out of Harvard to form Microsoft with Paul Allen.

In 1986, the Microsoft software company that Bill Gates had dropped out of Harvard to create went public, making Gates and Paul Allen overnight billionaires. By then, Microsoft didn't simply own and license the operating system for all IBM personal computers, but its operating system was also in virtually all the inexpensive IBM PC clones flooding the expanding market in the 1980s. And the second coming of Windows, in 1987, could run popular made-for-Mac programs like Excel, Word and Pagemaker. That was when the PC and its clones – cheaper than the Mac, if not as sophisticated, 'natural' or fast – became corporate America's standard.

The third version, Window 3.0, was released in 1990, and sold around ten million copies in two years. By the early 1990s a million copies of the company's Windows 3.1 software were being sold every single month, and the company was working on successors, code-named 'Chicago' and 'Cairo'. When Chicago came out in 1995, it was under the Windows 95 moniker; and in 2001, Cairo hit stores as Windows XP.

From the beginning, unlike some of its more hapless competitors, including those idealists who saw the Internet as a 'free', 'natural' resource, Microsoft always saw the advantages of being 'lawyered-up'. Perhaps it was simple prudence, given that from very early on its competitors accused Microsoft of being anti-competitive and monopoly-minded; perhaps it was the good influence of the elder Gates. In any event, Microsoft fought protracted, multi-year legal battles all through the 1980s – not only with Apple, which argued that Microsoft's reverse engineering of aspects of the Mac operating system amounted to copyright infringement, but with the PC clone manufacturers, who fought Microsoft's demands that they pay it licence fees for its operating system, whether they were using it or not. It fought well into the 1990s, too, with Netscape and others, often over the issue of 'bundling' Explorer, its Internet browser, with its operating software, while keeping its competitors out. All the while, as the rapidly expanding computer industry was sorting itself out, Microsoft kept growing.

Under the *laissez faire* Reagan and Bush the Elder administrations, regulators stood apart and let 'the market' do its work, and that meant that muscle and market share counted for everything in an exponentially burgeoning marketplace where computers – and the code that ran them – were changing the world.

In 2000, a US District Court judge ordered that Microsoft be broken up into two separate companies; a year later, that order was reversed on appeal. When the dust cleared, and the gavels came down for the last time, it was too late to stop mighty Microsoft. There were facts on the ground in the form of computers on every desk, and running in nearly each one...

Windows.

Flawed, patched, persistently hacked, but still the world's standard, running on more than 90 per cent of the world's personal computers.

In mid-1997, Microsoft stunned the computer industry by making a $150 million investment in Apple, giving it a 7 per cent nonvoting stake in its long-time arch-rival. When the announcement was made at the Macworld Expo trade show that year by Apple's Steve Jobs, appearing onstage, and by Gates, appearing by satellite, the audience of Mac partisans reacted with boos. The investment, cynics said, was simply a way for the giant software company to deflect anti-trust accusations.

Cynics reacted the same way in 2002 and 2003 when a neat bit of legal jujitsu turned what should have been anti-trust-settlement losses by Microsoft in class-action cases into still more opportunities for expanding its market share.

A decade ago Apple was the leader in educational sales to schools of computers, but its share of that lucrative market fell steadily to lower-priced PCs employing the Windows operating system. Then Microsoft, battling scores of private class-action lawsuits charging it with various anti-competitive practices, hit upon a novel two-for-one strategy to settle the suits out of court while further undermining Apple in that lucrative educational market: Microsoft's lawyers offered settlements that called for the company to donate hundreds of millions of dollars worth of its software to needy schools in California and elsewhere. All in all, Microsoft proposed to settle approximately 100 private class-action suits around the country in much that same way. What all the offers had in common is that, while they would put much-needed computer equipment into deserving schools, the settlements would at the very same time further erode Apple's educational market share.

Needless to say, Apple opposed the deals.

Today, Microsoft's biggest battles are still with lawyers and regulators, both in the United States and the European Union, who still want to see it broken up or restrained on anti-trust grounds. And at the end of March 2004, the European Union levied a record $600 million fine against the company for anti-trust violations.

Microsoft of course declared it would appeal.

At the beginning of April 2004, Microsoft again shocked the industry when it reached a surprise settlement with its long-time nemesis, Sun Microsystems, the Santa Clara, California-based computer company that created Java software and was the driving force behind both the American and European anti-trust cases against Microsoft. The bitter battle between the two technology giants was personal as well as professional, with CEO Scott McNealy, the generally acknowledged leader of the anti-Microsoft camp in American computing circles, deriding Gates as 'Darth Vader' and 'Butt-head', calling Microsoft the Evil Empire and Windows a 'hairball' of an operating system.

Sun, interestingly enough, had itself been struggling in recent years as cheaper competition, much of it running Windows, cut into its core corporate-server computers business. The settlement, in which Microsoft agreed to pay Sun $1,600,000,000, seemed to put all that in the past.

'Maybe we've grown up, and maybe they've grown up,' McNealy told *The New York Times*. The director of the Institute for the Future in Menlo Park, California, observed that the 'wheels of the legal system grind too slow to solve problems in the technology space'. Precisely. The best legal strategy then in the 'technology space' for an aggressive company with a head start in an emerging technology, is delay-delay-delay.

Although Microsoft long ago won the popularity war with Apple, it is still battling the greater 'intuitivity', as well as the perceived (and actual) superiority and reliability, of the Apple operating system. The next iteration of Windows, due in 2006 and code-named 'Longhorn', is expected to be Microsoft's answer to Apple's already existing OS-X.

Despite the billions that Microsoft paid out to its rival Sun and the hundreds of millions more it may yet pay out to the European Commission, the company still reported 'solid quarterly gains' in its revenue and operating income during the same period of the fine and payouts.

The company still maintained a monumental amount – more than $50 billion – in cash reserves, and it still provided its employees with free gym access and free beverages on the job. Around the same time, Microsoft advised analysts that, in its usual conservative estimation, its fiscal year 2005 revenue would be up about five per cent over 2004, to approximately $38 billion.

The news sent stock in the world's largest software company soaring.

Of course, while some Seattle kids of the time were getting buzzed on Starbucks, for others coffee was not remotely enough. Nothing was enough. From James Dean right on through to John Belushi, living very fast and dying very young has seemed as romantic as a Rimbaud poem to some hard-rocking, hard-living kids.

There he was, Kurt Cobain, just 27 years old and already in some quarters Seattle's favourite son, his haunted blue eyes framed by stringy blond hair, at the very height of his fame and influence; singing earnestly brutal rock songs about teen spirit and youthful alienation and anguish, and disdaining both record executives and fashionistas, who nonetheless loved the 'Corporate Rock Sucks' T-shirt and the rest of his charity shop clothes. His whole stance was that he despised anyone who saw him as an icon and wanted to make him famous, though he pursued it all the same.

Despite that, maybe because of it, the plaid flannel shirt that was the uniform of the Seattle grunge rock scene became an anti-fashion fashion sensation, the very emblem of Generation X.

Kurt Cobain was by far the biggest pop cultural influence ever to come out of Seattle's underground club scene. He was a talented, skinny kid with a chronically nervous stomach and an addiction to painkillers and heroin, who looked lost in his baggy wool sweater over torn jeans. In April 1994, reportedly after disappearing from a rehab clinic in Los Angeles, he went back to his home in Seattle, put a Remington 20-gauge shotgun to his head and pulled the trigger.

Two days later, an electrician went to the house to install an alarm system and discovered the body. Reportedly, Cobain's suicide note ended with a line quoting Neil Young, grunge's spiritual godfather: 'It is better to burn out than to fade away.'

It wasn't long before the inevitable conspiracy theories started. He was murdered, went the stories, by his wife, Courtney Love, or maybe by jealous fellow rockers, or by greedy family, or maybe in a drug deal gone bad. There was even a controversial documentary film, *Kurt & Courtney* (1998), about the accusations and the rumours surrounding his death.

'We bonded pharmaceutically over drugs,' his widow, actress-punk rocker Courtney Love, said of their attraction. She was a rock icon in her own right, the most notable and controversial female rocker to come out of the Seattle-based Riot Grrrl feminist rocker movement. Over the decade following Cobain's death she has remained a figure of persistent controversy. She has been arrested several times, and was recently charged with illegal possession of prescription painkillers, an accusation she disputes.

Hated and reviled, loved and admired, Courtney Love is also a figure of undeniable talent and charisma, both as a rocker and as an actress, winning several film critics' association awards for her work in the 1996 Milos Forman movie, *The People Versus Larry Flynt*, playing the wife of the American adult-magazine king. Unfortunately, in the wake of the legal charges, she has at least temporarily lost custody of the child she had with Cobain.

In April 2004 she reaped a bonanza of publicity – and a night in jail – promoting her latest Hole album, *America's Sweetheart*. Appearing on CBS's *The Late Show With David Letterman*, the irrepressible Ms Love leaped up on the host's desk and pulled up her blouse, exposing her breasts to the bemused host, who immediately thanked her.

The moment echoed another, similar, famous moment on the same show, when, on the occasion of David Letterman's birthday in the mid-'90s, actress Drew Barrymore also leapt up on the host's desk, did a little bump-and-grind and flashed her breasts, too.

'I can't thank you enough for that,' the host said then, too. 'I wish more of our guests would consider that.'

Almost a decade passed before that particular birthday wish came true. These days, Love seems equal parts Hollywood bombshell, grunge-rock chick and 'napalm feminist' (as Helene A Shugart, an assistant professor at the University of Utah, characterised her). Clearly Courtney likes the spotlight and plays at being outrageous. But is it really still the pharmaceuticals? Ms Love says no.

Later the same night, Courtney was photographed outside a Manhattan fast-food restaurant, letting a grinning total stranger nuzzle her bare breast. And still later in the night, she performed an impromptu set at Plaid, the East Village club of the moment. During one number, she allegedly threw a microphone stand into the audience, injuring a fan. Inadvertent, her spokespersons said. The New York police were not amused, and Courtney Love was arrested, charged with reckless endangerment and spent the night in jail at the Ninth Precinct in the East Village.

'Now he's gone and joined that stupid club,' Kurt Cobain's mother told the Associated Press a few days after he died, referring to rock stars like Jim Morrison and Jimi Hendrix, who'd overdosed and died a senseless early death. 'I told him not to join that stupid club.'

'I feel stupid and contagious', he'd howled in Nirvana's most famous song on the album *Nevermind*, which sold ten million copies worldwide. The raw, abrasive chorus spoke to the hopelessness and cynicism of Generation X, the younger generation that came after the Baby Boomers. It was something else 'Made in America' – a sound and a sensibility – that kids around the world could understand.

In the US, Gen X was the generation that feared its future would be reduced to a life in the more numerous Boomers' shadows, dining on their cultural and economic scraps. Populations around the world – in India, Asia, South America and the Middle East – were growing younger, and a lot of those kids felt their futures didn't look so bright, too. They, too, could relate to his songs:

'Here we are now/Entertain us/A mulatto/An albino/A mosquito/My Libido/Yeah, a denial/A denial/A denial.'

There was no denying his death, though, just as there was no denying the worldwide impact of the handful of albums Nirvana released, including *Nevermind* and *In Utero*, before Kurt Cobain pulled the trigger.

4 San Francisco: Sex, Drugs, The Rise Of Youth Culture (And Personal Liberation Movements)

'What're you rebelling against, Johnny?'

'Whaddya got?'

When young Marlon Brando, playing the slouching, smouldering, sensitive tough-guy leader of the Black Rebels motorcycle gang in the influential 1953 cult film *The Wild One*, delivered that memorable movie line, Altamont was still 16 years away.

The Wild One was one of the first pictures made for the newly discovered 'teen' audience. It was considered shocking in its time (and was even banned in Britain for some years), presumably because of its depiction of an amoral, outlaw 'youth culture' – the gang of swaggering bikers who took over and terrorised a small American town.

The film, in fact, was based on a true incident. During the 4 July weekend in 1947, some 4,000 motorcyclists roared into the sleepy little town of Hollister, California, about 145km (90 miles) south of San Francisco, for a weekend of partying that turned violent. An article in *Harper's* magazine, entitled 'The Cyclists' Raid', recounted the wild, lawless weekend that terrified the little country town, and that became the basis of the film.

Director Stanley Kramer, known for making prestigious 'social issue' films, such as *On The Beach* and *Judgment At Nuremberg*, told his biographer that he and Brando had researched the picture by talking to actual bikers, and that much of the dialogue came directly from them, including the film's most famous line. 'I asked one of the kids, "What are you rebelling against?"' Kramer recalled, 'and he answered, "What have you got?"'

In the '50s, the line – and the film, and all the other teen films that came after it, from *Rebel Without A Cause* to *Rock, Rock, Rock* – resonated not just with American kids, growing up in the suburbs and dreaming about hot rods, but with kids all around the world.

At the end of the '60s, Altamont came to be synonymous with the biggest and most public of youth-culture bad trips. It was the name of the 'speedway' south of San Francisco that was the inauspicious site of the Rolling Stones free concert that put an end to the media-fuelled idea that the sex, drugs 'n' rock 'n' roll youth culture of the long-haired 'hippies' was a harmless and groovy idyll. The word 'hippie' itself was a reporter-coined term that was a play on the earlier generation of 'hipsters', who also were drawn to San Francisco and the Bay Area, and who created their own counter-culture around so-called 'cool' jazz, spoken poetry and the 'beat' ethic, man. The media frenzy around the hippies began with what came to be known as the San Francisco Summer of Love two and a half years before, in 1967. A saccharine pop song immortalised that brief Peter Max period, when it seemed like the new era of perpetually blue skies and rainbow possibilities was imminent: 'If you're going to San Francisco', the lyric urged would-be hippies, 'be sure to wear some flowers in your hair.'

However, the flower-garlanded noggins of the 'heads', as the drug-taking hippies were also known at the time, stood little chance against the pool cue-wielding Hells Angels, the biker club that for most people best personified Brando's 'whaddya got' charismatic bad-boy image.

At that December 1969 Altamont free concert, which was filmed for the documentary film *Gimme Shelter*, hulking Hells Angels, hired as 'security' for the Stones, stabbed an 18-year-old Black man, Meredith Hunter, to death in front of the low stage while, just a few feet away, Mick Jagger sang 'Under My Thumb'.

The Angels' idea of crowd control was wading into the audience crowded up front, swinging pool cues and throwing fists. They even knocked out one of the singers in the Jefferson Airplane, one of the Bay Area bands that performed at the free concert, when he tried to stop another fight.

The bad trip that was Altamont took place only a few months after the original 'peace 'n' love' Woodstock music festival, and 'Altamont' has become shorthand for the moment when a generation of kids lost their innocence, not to mention their faith in the disarming power of peace 'n' love.

Of course, between the so-called Summer of Love and the so-called Altamont Death Trip, there were the inner-city riots of 1967, the Robert Kennedy and Martin Luther King political assassinations and the riots and anti-war demonstrations of 1968 – as well as the Manson murders in Los Angeles, the Stonewall Inn riot in New York (in which seething drag queens in a gay bar fought the police, launching the Gay Liberation movement) and the first manned landing on the moon, all in 1969. These incidents were all part of the trippy, deadly, roller-coaster carnival-sideshow ride that was America in the Vietnam era.

The music lasted, but the hippie utopia quickly turned out to be just a smoke dream.

The Altamont moment also put an end to the unlikely alliance between the flower-bedecked hippies, who smoked pot and opposed the war in Vietnam, and the Angels, tough pro-war bikers who liked their mind-altering substances cold, in crushable aluminium cans. But despite those kind of fissures among its outcasts and dropouts, for most of the period between the early '50s of Brando and the late '60s of Jagger, it was San Francisco that was, arguably, the epicentre of the whole turned-on, tuned-in, with-it world.

America gave the world the idea of rebellious teenagers, taking refuge from clueless adults in their very own culture, with their very own fashions, music and movies, but it was one American city in particular that showed the world how enticing and thrilling (and dangerous) that culture looked in practice.

Whether it was the Summer of Love or Altamont, or the great Gay Marriage Spree of our own Governator's time, San Francisco has long been synonymous with America's live-and-let-live ethos – and the quest for personal liberation – that the rest of the world finds so appealing. And from a distance, even the danger looks good.

Perhaps San Francisco's hospitality to all things new and trendy, to outcasts and visionaries, is a matter of Baghdad by the Bay's own buccaneering history. Social critics of that history have always regarded the city as louche and brazen, like some leering barker outside a North Beach strip club. But perhaps the city's c'est-la-vie attitude toward the harsher realities is just a halo effect of the Bay's physical beauty and unsurpassed, temperate Mediterranean clime. Then again, perhaps it's part of the fatalism that comes simply from living on the fault line.

Situated on a fog-shrouded peninsula some 1,287km (800 miles) south of Seattle, San Francisco is built on a series of steep and rolling hills that overlook the Pacific Ocean and the San Francisco Bay. The entire Bay Area, of which it is the hub, is, in fact, a place of great physical beauty and mostly temperate micro-climates, though Mark Twain, the ex-riverboat pilot and ex-prospector, who spent two years in the 1860s knocking around the city and writing colourful little stories for various local newspapers, was once supposed to have said, 'The coldest winter I ever saw was the summer I spent in San Francisco.'

Ironically enough, given that the city continues to this day to be one of the major trans-shipment points for northern California's thriving black-market marijuana-growing industry, it originally grew out of a tiny settlement called Yerba Buena, which means 'good herb'. It's a name the city lives up to, to the present day.

San Francisco remained a sleepy little backwater with only some 200 full-time residents until 1848, the year gold was discovered at Sutter's Mill on the south fork of the American River. At a stroke, fortune hunters from all over the world began to pour into the little city, stocking up on supplies, most likely doing some boozing and whoring, before heading off for the gold fields to the west, and a lawless enclave called the Barbary Coast sprang up on the San Francisco waterfront. It was a haven for opium dens, houses of prostitution and gambling palaces, a fog-shrouded warren where unsuspecting sailors could be enticed into a dark alley, snatched and 'shanghaied'.

That was the San Francisco that Mark Twain knew. He hadn't yet made his literary reputation, but his dispatches, filled with accounts of rascals and criminals and the public disputes of the boisterous city's day, gave a good account of the rowdiness and rough-and-tumble of the teeming, scheming city.

Twain duly reported on the nefarious doings of a gang that recruited young girls into prostitution, plying them with obscene books and pictures, both girls from good families and 'baldheads', as scandalously unbonneted street girls were called at the time.

He reported as well on a young woman who had falsely accused a 'hackman' (that is, the driver of a horse-drawn carriage) of raping her. She 'had a notion to halloo, when [the hackman] was about taking undue liberties with her', Twain wrote, 'but she sought a refuge and assuaged her grief that night at the Portsmouth Hotel, in the embraces of a benevolent person with whom she had met for the first time that day. He protected her injured innocence until seven o'clock the next morning, when she sallied forth to seek another protector. The case,' Twain noted dryly, 'was discharged.'

Twain had moved on by the time the transcontinental railroad arrived in San Francisco at the end of the 1860s. The city's famous cable cars were introduced a few years later. By the turn of the century, picturesque little San Francisco was a thriving American metropolis with a somewhat titillating, somewhat scandalous reputation.

Then, early on the morning of 18 April 1906, disaster struck. The Great San Francisco Earthquake killed more than 500 people. The fires that followed devastated 10sq km (4sq m) of the central city.

Of course, some among the censorious and self-righteous thought the city had it coming. As a popular song of the time had it, 'God spanked the city for being over-frisky.'

'Of all the Sodoms and Gomorrahs in our modern world, it is the worst,' *fin-de-siècle* American literary curmudgeon Ambrose Bierce fumed a year later. 'It needs another quake… That moral penal colony of the world!'

But the destroyed city rebuilt. And in the 1930s, while the entire country struggled through the Great Depression, it built the Golden Gate and Bay Bridges, the massive public works projects that have come to symbolise it.

In the 1940s, San Francisco became one of the main ports of departure for American forces heading to war in the Pacific Theater. So cosmopolitan had once-unruly San Francisco become that after World War II it was the site where the nations of the world gathered to adopt the charter creating the United Nations.

By the 1950s, while the rest of the country mostly drowsed through the middle-of-the-road Eisenhower years, experimentation and openness in both arts and lifestyles remained solidly part of the city's avant-garde image. The city thought of itself as a lighthouse, calling out to the young and the disaffected, all through the comfortable fog of Eisenhower-era prosperity and conformity.

Every bit as much as teeming, polyglot New York, the City by the Bay was regarded as a refuge from the suburban mainstream world. It became the mecca for the 'beats' and for hip musicians, most especially the jazz players, of all types.

In the 1960s, temperate, tolerant San Francisco naturally embraced the hippies.

The rise of the hippies, the young, long-haired shock troops of the youth culture, was a simple matter of predictable demographics. For the most part, 'hippies' were just teenage kids addicted to *epater les bourgeois* outrageousness, convinced the adult world was uncool, untrustworthy and corrupt – not so surprising in a young cohort in wartime, whose members were subject to the military draft.

A 'cohort' is what social scientists and others call a distinct group; in this case, the cohort was composed of the vast numbers of post-war kids, many born to returning World War II veterans, almost all born within the space of a few years. The media took to calling them the Baby Boomers, and they comprised the biggest single cohort in American history.

It was the first generation raised with a TV in the house. And in the sixties they became teenagers and then set off for college – or at least for the college towns where the 'cohort' congregated, and the 'vibe' was 'mellow'. Back then, nowhere could boast a mellower vibe than the Bay Area, where even the hazy sunshine had a mellow, golden glow. Some young Boomers had high hopes and others were just hoping to get high.

From the vantage point of the 21st century, it's easy to scoff at the San Francisco '60s – to snigger knowingly at the long hair, the tie-dyed T-shirts, the granny glasses and the Nehru jackets; at the utter conviction that recreational drugs were benign (amazingly enough, even including methamphetamine and cocaine); that anyone over 30 was not to be trusted and that revolution in America was for sure, man, on its way.

Whatever you want to say about those kids, they did put sex, drugs and rock 'n' roll on the American cultural map, where despite the best efforts of the country's moral guardians they remain to this day (even if these days the sex requires a condom, the drugs are apt to be tranquillisers, steroids or even Viagra, and today's emblematic rock 'n' roller might just be a hot little Pop Tart). But there was more. Strip away the dated trappings and the idealistic, simplistic, jejune convictions and consider what else really happened.

In 1964, just past the Sather Gate at the end of Telegraph Avenue in Berkeley, the little college town nestled along the foot of the Oakland hills, across the Bay and facing downtown San Francisco, the Free Speech Movement (FSM) was born on the University of California campus.

The Movement began as a response to the administration's peremptory ban, in September of that year, against 'advocative literature and activities on off-campus political issues' on a specific 8m- (26ft)-long strip of University property near the Sather Gate entrance. That was where student activists, of all stripes, traditionally had gathered, setting up folding tables, handing out literature and advocating passionately for and against 'off-campus political issues', like racism, Communism and workers' rights.

That misbegotten attempt at campus censorship came at just the wrong time for the university administration. UC Berkeley students were active already in opposition to McCarthyism, the late-'50s anti-Communist witch hunt, and they were also actively supporting the unionising activities of poor, mostly Black, hotel workers, some of them in the posh Nob Hill hotels of San Francisco.

It was right at the beginning of a period of rising campus social activism, and all the activists of all the tiny groups, many in opposition to each other, came together under the inclusive umbrella of the FSM. And to everyone's amazement, huge crowds of students began to gather on the plaza near the Gate, day after day. There they listened to folk music and agitprop, as well as to one very compelling student speaker who made a very compelling case:

'There's a time when the operation of the machine becomes so odious, makes you so sick at heart, that you can't take part,' the late Mario Savio (1942–96), the philosophy and physics student who emerged as the FSM's most fiery public speaker, told a crowd on the Sproul Plaza in December of that year. 'Put your bodies upon the gears! Upon the wheels! Upon the levers! Upon all the apparatus! You've got to make it stop!'

His speech electrified the student crowd, which set out to do just as Mister Savio suggested. And that night, police arrested some 800 of the protesters in what was then the largest mass arrest in California history.

As kids around the world watched in amazement, the Berkeley students succeeded in shutting the vast university down. Those large and generally peaceful 'sit-ins' in campus administration offices and the mass demonstrations throughout the autumn of 1964 became the inspiration and the model for, and the organisational nucleus of, the anti-war movement of the second half of the 1960s, as well as of the women's and gay liberation movements of the early '70s.

Earlier, in the summer of 1964, Mario Savio had gone to the American South to help register Black voters as part of the Student Nonviolent Coordinating Committee's (SNCC) Mississippi Summer Project.

SNCC had been formed in 1960 by Black college students, and it was in the vanguard of the sit-in movement, during which courageous young Blacks 'sat' at segregated facilities, such as Whites-only lunch counters. By the summer of 1964, SNCC had joined with the New York-based Congress of Racial Equality on so-called Freedom Rides, dangerous bus trips through the segregated South, during which the Freedom Riders used segregated public facilities, including restaurants and restrooms on the bus routes.

Mario Savio was one of approximately 600 young people, both White and Black, who went to Mississippi to register new Black voters. It was courageous and it was dangerous. In June of that year, three young Mississippi Summer-project activists – two young Whites and one young Black – were murdered by members of the Ku Klux Klan.

In Mississippi, Savio saw at first hand the philosophy and tactics of non-violent protest practised by the Civil Rights Movement. Those tactics had been adopted, generally, by Martin Luther King from the non-violent campaign that Mohandas Gandhi waged against the British in India. They also became the tactics of the Berkeley Free Speech Movement, and then of the opponents of the Vietnam War, the women who pressed for equal rights and the homosexual men who put gay rights on the national agenda.

Gay rights were controversial at first, even more controversial as far as the moral guardians were concerned than women's rights. But throughout all the years of turmoil, San Francisco remained a gay mecca and a mecca of tolerance for free thinkers of all sexual orientations.

San Francisco was a mecca for the music of the '60s too. And the man who was responsible not only for much of the emblematic music of the psychedelic '60s, but for the psychedelic look of the period, too, was an immigrant from Berlin named Wolfgang Granjonca.

Raised in orphanages and foster homes, Granjonca arrived in the United States at the age of ten and grew up in a foster home in the Bronx. Turning 18, he changed his name to Bill Graham (a name he picked out of a phone book), joined the military, went to Korea, arrived back and made his way to San Francisco, where he became friends with members of the politically and socially active San Francisco Mime Troupe.

It was then he discovered his knack for organising big, complex events that would take him to the pinnacle of American popular music: Bill Graham, it turned out, was a whiz of a concert promoter.

His first concert was a mid-'60s benefit for the San Francisco Mime Troupe, which put on free, politically oriented plays in the Brechtian tradition in the local parks. The Troupe had been charged with obscenity after one performance, and the Graham benefit came to the rescue. The night and the music it produced have become legendary. On the bill were Frank Zappa And The Mothers Of Invention, Jefferson Airplane and The Fugs, as well as Beat poets Lawrence Ferlinghetti and Allen Ginsburg.

At his three-day Trips Festival a few months later, whirling light shows and many of San Francisco's emerging 'acid rock' bands were on the bill, as was the psychedelic lysergic acid that inspired them. The new Bay bands included Quicksilver Messenger Service, Country Joe And The Fish and Big Brother And The Holding Company.

It was Graham's organisation that innovated the strobe lighting, the colourful kaleidoscopic projected patterns, and the slides and movies projected on a screen above the stage that became indispensable accompaniments to the long, free-form riffs and acid rock that later were on the regular bill at his concert hall, the Fillmore West.

From the Fillmore West to the Fillmore East in New York, from the Trips Festival to Live Aid, the former Mister Granjonca, who died in a helicopter crash in 1991, was the consummate impresario of rock's psychedelic era.

In 1967, a San Francisco FM deejay, Tom Donahue – now regarded as the father of so-called underground radio – began playing great, eclectic blocks of music that reflected his own tastes, from funk and rock to experimental jazz, rather than a playlist that was pre-conceived and pre-ordained from on high.

The deejay's simple innovation became popular, speaking as it did to the '60s' psychedelic sense of connection among all things, including styles of music. The San Francisco trend caught on nationally, and for the next few years FM radio became an unparalleled place to find new music and develop new musical tastes. Then a first wave of corporate conglomeration in the '70s radio business meant the return of the exclusionary format and the rigid playlist, and the end of the FM deejay's brief heyday as a musical master of ceremonies.

The same year that underground radio began broadcasting the long, jazzy cuts and the psychedelic sounds of young musicians steeped in the era's drug culture, 200,000 or so hippies and other young seekers floated down the highway from San Francisco and the surrounding Bay Area for three days of rock at the Monterey Pop Festival. The festival featured breakout performances by soon-to-be '60s emblems who then were relative unknowns, including Jimi Hendrix, Janis Joplin and Laura Nyro, as well as such established youth-culture stars of the period as The Who, Grateful Dead, and Simon And Garfunkel.

A little more than a year later, the youth culture finally got its own media voice. When San Francisco-based *Rolling Stone* magazine went to press with its first issue, its founder/editor was an ambitious 21 year old named Jann Wenner. The new magazine, he said, would not be just about the music 'but also about the things and attitudes that the music embraces'.

The same year that *Rolling Stone* first rolled off the presses, the counter-culture spread into the mainstream in two big ways. First, tens of thousands of demonstrators gathered in Chicago, during the Democratic national political convention, and fought pitched battles with baton- and tear-gas-wielding police on the streets. 'The whole world is watching!' they chanted, while television cameras recorded the events.

Then *Hair*, the musical about letting the Aquarian sunshine in, about hippies, getting stoned and finding true love and going off to Vietnam, as well as about all those naked young hard bodies up onstage, opened on Broadway. It was, sniffed the critics, a sell-out in more ways than one. And many of those critics were back in San Francisco, where disaffected militants – hippies, gays, women – were keeping the true counter-cultural faith alive.

In those years, the Bay Area was a major centre of the women's liberation movement. The National Organization For Women (NOW) had been formed in 1966 in Washington DC with the aim of changing laws and of securing equal rights, equal pay and the like. The 'women's liberation' movement, on the other hand, was less formally structured and in its early years consisted of smaller, ad-hoc 'consciousness-raising' groups of young, college-educated women, self-described feminists who often employed the language of psychotherapy and used political theatre and public confrontation to address issues of domestic relationships, sexuality and personal freedom. Many of women's liberation's earliest consciousness-raising groups in the Bay Area, such as the fancifully named Sudsofloppen, Gallstones and Red Witch, included veterans of the free-speech, anti-war and civil rights movements. They protested bridal fairs and beauty contests, and conducted guerilla-theatre 'ogle-ins', in which they stared at and commented on men's bodies.

Those were the years when the Bay Area was all about protests, about pushing the envelope and shocking public displays. They were also about disco and glam rock, about hard drugs and hard partying.

The most famous San Francisco gay bathhouses of the period had weekly coed nights. Meanwhile, drag performers in San Francisco organised into a popular gender-bending satirical theatrical troupe called The Cockettes, and for a time they seemed to symbolise Baghdad by the Bay.

The Cockettes were all about glitter and gowns, flouncing and tottering around onstage in impossibly high platform shoes. They were about big hair, big breasts and equally big beards. It was camp, and San Francisco was a beacon that spoke to the world: here is a place where anything goes.

In the years after the Vietnam War finally ended, what happened was what has always happened after wars, whether the United States was involved or not (and has happened after famines and pogroms and other large-scale calamities): tens of thousands of immigrants streamed into the United States. This time they were Vietnamese, Cambodian and Laotian refugees, and they crowded into the cities and towns all along the West Coast, where the Chinatowns and Little Tokyos were soon joined by bustling Little Saigons and Little Phnom Penhs.

The refugees arriving in the country were voting with their feet, heading directly to the US, where things might be tough, and life might be a struggle, but at least there was hope. Then, as the '70s turned into the '80s, vicious guerilla wars across Central America filled the Little El Salvadors and Little Guatemalas in California cities, too, where the impoverished immigrants packed in small apartments might work long hours cutting lawns, clearing tables and washing dishes or sewing designer clothes, but their children just might find themselves living in peace and plenty; in short, living an American Dream.

By the turn of the millennium, the population of San Francisco County, for example, was just over 50 per cent minorities, including over 30 per cent Asian. Over 49 per cent of San Franciscans were female, and just over 28 per cent and 35 per cent of the businesses in the county were owned by women and minorities, respectively. How does that compare with what you see around you?

Around a 45-minute drive south of San Francisco on Highway 101 is the Santa Clara Valley, a place whose industry has arguably done more to advance the cause of personal liberation than any of the grand '-isms' of the 20th century. In the process of advancing that noble cause many people also got very, very rich. Could there be anything more all-American than that?

The Valley of Heart's Delight, as the Santa Clara Valley was called a hundred years ago, when it was known for its abundant fruit orchards, is today a place of rolling hills dotted by black oaks and coast live oaks, of lush vineyards and leafy suburbs, of liveable little cities and sprawling office parks.

Nowadays, the name most people know the Valley by is, of course, Silicon Valley. Where once there were fruit orchards now there are companies with names like Apple, Cisco Systems, eBay, Hewlett-Packard, Intel, Intuit, Oracle and Yahoo!

Most histories of Silicon Valley go back to the legendary day in 1939 when Stanford University classmates Bill Hewlett and Dave Packard tossed a coin to see whose name would go first in their new company, whose first product, a resistance-capacitance audio oscillator, was built in a Palo Alto, California, garage. H-P 200A, the oscillator was shrewdly designated, so potential buyers might conclude it was the latest version of an existing line. One of the earliest customers for that oscillator was The Walt Disney Company, which purchased 8 of the devices to develop and test the new sound system that was being installed in 12 theatres showing Disney's 1940 animated musical extravaganza *Fantasia*.

At the end of Hewlett-Packard's first year of operation, revenue was all of $5,369. By the end of the 20th century, H-P, by then a giant computing, printing and imaging corporation, had annual revenues of $42 billion.

Histories of the Valley point, too, to the seminal day in the early 1950s when Stanford University, then in need of some cash, created the Stanford Industrial Park. H-P became one of the office park's earliest tenants.

As important as Stanford University and the pioneers of H-P were to the history of the Silicon Valley, the true tipping point in its history probably came almost two decades after the company's founding there, according to Martin Kenney, a University of California professor who edited Stanford University Press's *Understanding Silicon Valley: The Anatomy Of An Entrepreneurial Region*. That was when the Fairchild Semiconductor company 'happened to locate there. The company spawned dozens of "Fairchildren" nearby, building the fundamental engines of the digital revolution,' according to a *Newsweek* magazine report about academic studies that focused on the digital revolution.

In fact, soon more than two dozen semiconductor-related firms were started, most of them in the Valley, by former Fairchild employees.

How important was centring the semiconductor industry in the Valley? Consider that silicon, the basic ingredient in sand, is among the best materials for semiconducting, and that 'computer chips, both for CPU and memory, are composed of semiconductor materials', as well as the fact that 'semiconductors make it possible to miniaturize electronic components, such as transistors', as the Nanoelectronics website puts it. The first integrated circuit, a complete electric circuit on a single chip, came out of Fairchild's labs, too.

The post-World War II history of Silicon Valley is a story of technological invention and of entrepreneurial growth, of fortunes made and lost, and of boyish-looking buccaneers dressed in khakis, windbreakers and running shoes, their outfits accessorised by plastic pocket protectors and backpacks, becoming overnight billionaires.

The creation of Fairchild, which was formed by a group of employees from Shockley Transistor, another electronics company (and also a tenant of the Stanford Industrial Park), was a template for what became almost the Silicon Valley company creation myth. 'A small coterie of employees in a firm, dissatisfied with their current place of employment, would gather after work to tinker around with some of their own ideas,' historian Paul Mackun said in *Computer Weekly*. 'They would then develop a business plan, acquire funds from venture capitalists and seek advice from local academic sources. If they succeeded, they were heroes.'

In those early post-war years, the Silicon Valley was fuelled by Defense Department and National Aeronautics And Space Administration (NASA) dollars. For example, the government bought 100 per cent of all integrated circuits produced in 1962, according to a 2001 article in *Business History Review*. By 1965, the government's share had dropped to 72 per cent and, by 1968, it was a mere 37 per cent of the year's total shipment of integrated circuits.

In the period from the bombing of Pearl Harbor to the election of JFK as president, over 400,000 jobs, many in the electronics industry, were created in Santa Clara County. Between 1960 and 1975, the county's employment rate grew a blistering 156 per cent, compared to 65 per cent for the state of California and 46 per cent for the country as a whole, according to data quoted in the *Business History Review* essay. However, because Silicon Valley was in America, not in the Soviet Union and not, say, in North Korea, those techno-geeks and high-tech entrepreneurs who populated the Valley in the post-war years, meeting the technology needs of Defense and NASA, were free to make their fortunes, too, to hook up with venture capitalists looking to make money by funding consumer applications for all those nifty micro-electronic devices.

As time went by, the PC and the Internet, not to mention Tang and Teflon, were spun off to average consumers, and all those IPO (initial public offering) billionaires in the late '80s and the '90s were created.

The ethos in the Valley in the boom time was electric...in more ways than one. 'A good contract is not sealed with a drink anymore, but with a line of coke,' said no less an authority on the subject of crime in Silicon Valley than the Chief of Police of San José, California. And for the biggest part of two decades, as real-estate prices doubled and tripled, the good times rolled on and on.

Of course, the dotcom bubble that burst one fine spring day at the turn of the millennium hit Silicon Valley especially hard, but at least in retrospect it seemed inevitable in the way it mirrored the growth pattern of other industries based on world-changing technologies. In the early days of the auto industry, for example, literally hundreds of car manufacturers vied for what obviously was becoming a vast and lucrative new market. Then came the inevitable shakeout. After the dust cleared only a handful of auto manufacturers were left clustered in Detroit, which became to the auto industry (Motor City) what the Santa Clara Valley (Silicon Valley) is to high tech.

'There have been two thousand automobile brands in America and there [are] only two left – General Motors and Ford,' Al Ries, chairman of Ries & Ries, an Atlanta-based marketing consultancy, told *Darwin* magazine at the height of the dotcom meltdown. 'That doesn't mean the automobile business is a lousy business just because nineteen hundred and ninety-eight companies went out of the automobile business. No, every new business is that way.'

Predictably, prospects for all those Asian, Indian and White all-American entrepreneurs have brightened again in the Valley. One typical software entrepreneur, thirty-two-year-old Bill Nguyen, told *Forbes* magazine early in 2004 that he just isn't going 'to hold back anymore', and in classic Silicon Valley form he shelled out $40,000 of his own money for a party to celebrate the return of the good times. If his eight–five employees can increase the company's revenues by 40 per cent this year, he said, he'll treat them all to a week's vacation in Hawaii.

Possibly the biggest sign of all that the bubble is beginning to reinflate is the excitement surrounding the planned IPO of a six-year-old search-engine company whose name has become a verb.

Google was started in traditional Silicon Valley fashion in 1998 – in the requisite Palo Alto garage – by Larry Page and Sergey Brin, two Stanford University graduate students who, according to company legend, max'd out their credit cards to buy their first terrabyte of memory and set up their first data centre in Page's dorm room. By the middle of the next year, the Valley's most prominent venture capitalists, including John Doerr of Kleiner Perkins Caufield & Byers and Mike Moritz of Sequoia, invested $12.5 million each for stakes in Google (that will probably be worth at least $6 billion if the company goes public, as currently expected). By making the investment, the two long-time venture capitalists, whose earlier picks had included Sun Microsytems, Intuit, Amazon and Yahoo!, were then entitled to seats around the legendary ping-pong table that served as the first conference table for Google's board.

The Google IPO is expected to net anywhere between $15–45 billion and to make multi-billionaires of the two founders. Sceptics and critics run the gamut from those who think Microsoft may attack (there are others, of course, who think it's Microsoft that should be worried) to those who think the two founders aren't practical enough businessmen, because they've 'talked about building space transporters and implanting chips in people's heads that can provide them with information as they think'.

Of course, the Google founders are not the only Internet-era moguls to think deep-space thoughts. Microsoft's cofounder Paul Allen is the financier behind SpaceShipOne, a reusable manned rocket-powered space plane, privately developed, that's already flown to an altitude of some 100km (62 miles) on a suborbital flight over the Mojave Desert. That flight marked the advent of privately financed space travel. And, if you're keeping track of such things, that flight also made the United States the first country in which a kid actually grew up to own his own space-faring rocket ship.

There are also those who think going public will wilt the unique, exuberant corporate culture Page and Brin created at Google, which has given rise to so much innovation. Here's how the company itself describes that corporate culture in the early days, way back at the turn of the millennium:

'To maximize the flexibility of the work space, large rubber exercise balls were re-purposed as highly mobile office chairs in an open environment free of cubicle walls. While computers on the desktops were fully powered, the desks themselves were wooden doors held up by pairs of sawhorses. Lava lamps began sprouting like multi-hued mushrooms. Large dogs roamed the halls.... After a rigorous review process, Charlie Ayers was hired as company chef, bringing with him an eclectic repertoire of health-conscious recipes he developed while cooking for the Grateful Dead. Sections of the parking lot were roped off for twice-weekly roller hockey games.'

Is this not the very vision of those flower-garlanded San Francisco hippies dancing ecstatically to the Dead at the Trips Festival in the mid-'60s? Is this not the workplace of the candy-coloured play-time-all-the-time American Dream?

5 Seventh Avenue: How The Rag Trade Became Haute Couture

What was once the ideal of French sophistication and glamour has evolved into yet another big engine of the American pop culture machine. The reason?

In America, traditionally, anyone who could afford a sewing machine and a few bolts of fabric could become a clothing manufacturer. And today, anyone with a good hand for sketching, who can afford a sketchbook and drawing pencils, can become a designer.

The 'rag trade' has always been a gateway industry for immigrants without much cash but with a drive to succeed, with a hunger perhaps for fortune and fame, which drives them to pursue their vision of American style and the American Dream. The story of how the humble garment district spawned the super-model glamour of Fashion Week is, in short, another tale of ambitious immigrants in humble circumstances dreaming big American dreams.

Of course, fashion has existed ever since Eve, alarmed by her nakedness, looked around at what the Garden had to offer and picked out that fig leaf. The ancient Egyptians had one uniform for slaves and another for their overseers; the classical Greeks had a wardrobe that consisted of flowing robes, short tunics and longer chitons; the Romans had their designer togas. When Louis XIV ruled France, the ever more elaborate fashions of his court were followed slavishly by his courtiers and enviously by the rest of Europe. In fact, the artful, ever-changing and ever more elaborate designs, the expensive fabrics, the bejewelled and beribboned costumes, the plumed hats and outrageously ornate wigs were in effect a shrewd way to bind the French nobles to their kings and queens, who also were their undisputed fashion leaders. And this French domination of fashion for the nobility of all European nations continued right up until the time of the Revolution.

It took Robespierre and the Reign of Terror – when mere possession of a gown fit for a ball at the palace might cost its owner her head – to make fashion statements mortally dangerous. In Republican France, that lasted until Napoleon declared himself Emperor and made it safe for the upper classes to dress like the aristos they were again.

In 1846, in the first decade of the Victorian era, an Englishman, Charles Frederick Worth, arrived in Paris and began the kind of custom dressmaking for the court of Napoleon III, presided over by his elegant and fashionable wife, the Empress Eugénie, that later became known as haute couture, or 'high fashion'. That same year, in the United States, the first patent was issued for the sewing machine. It was an important milestone of the Industrial Revolution, because it led to dressmaking and tailoring for the rising new middle classes of mercantilism. At around the same time, the advent of photography also meant that an avid middle-class audience in both Britain and the United States existed not only for fashionable clothes, but for illustrated fashion magazines. The era of machine-made and ready-to-wear clothes for the masses with some disposable money began.

Of course, the sewing machine led in short order to the rise of the sweatshop. That was particularly true in New York City, already by then a teeming American metropolis filled with immigrants crowded into tenements. The Jews from eastern Europe and the Italians from the south of Europe pouring off the ships in the docks of Lower Manhattan didn't need to know the language, or even to be particularly skilful or dexterous, to do piece work for $4 (£2.50) per week, bent over clattering Singers in poorly lit and unventilated factories on the Lower East Side.

Around the same time, on the other side of the continent, a German immigrant was changing the world of fashion, although it would be a hundred years and more before that change swept up from the streets and out of the factories and became the mark of young American style.

In 1853, Levi Strauss, a native of Bavaria, immigrated to America and travelled to San Francisco, where he set about making sturdy clothing with copper rivets for the gold miners who had gone West during the Gold Rush. It was his inspiration to make those 'waist overalls', as they were known, out of thick denim, a twill-weave cotton. Denim is said to derive from *serge de Nimes*, a French fabric dating back to the 1700s, while the term 'jean' originally referred to a sturdy Italian cotton blend from Genoa that dates to the 1600s and was sometimes used for uniforms worn by Italian sailors. And so, in an American reformulation, the humble blue jean was born. It remained humble work clothing until the 1930s, when cowboy movie stars like John Wayne began wearing denim jeans, and World War II, when jeans became part of the work uniform both for young sailors and their girlfriends back home.

When America entered the war, the young men went off to fight and the young women took off their aprons and marched off to work in what was then called the Arsenal of Democracy, taking their places on the assembly lines in the plants and factories that were turning out the planes, the tanks, the ships and the bombs needed to fight the world war. The archetype of the young working women in those wartime days was hailed as 'Rosie the Riveter'.

Many of the six million plus young women inside the factories and in the shipyards on the homefront began wearing jeans, too. Meanwhile, young designers in New York, deprived of other materials by wartime rationing, began using denim for skirts and jackets. At the end of the war, Levi's began selling its waist overalls outside of the American West for the first time, and demand for them extended to Europe, where off-duty GIs had worn theirs.

Hollywood also spread denim's new cachet: Brando in *The Wild One*, James Dean in *Rebel Without A Cause* and Carol Lynley and Brandon De Wilde as the teenage lovers in *Blue Denim* (a 1959 exploitation movie, shocking for its time, that included a teen pregnancy and an illegal backroom abortionist) made the one-time San Francisco miner's uniform hip. In due course fashion designers made the material expensive.

Today, jeans are an $11 billion a year business, and modish folks with money can spend up to $280 for a single pair of stylish jeans from such makers as Blue Guru, Chip and Pepper, Citizens of Humanity, Earl, G-Star, Habitual, James, Miss Sixty, Notify, Paper Denim & Cloth, Rogan, Saddlelite, Seven for All Mankind and Diesel, which originated both the 'dirty denim' jean look and the whole idea of 'premium' jeans.

It's a long way from the rough-and-tumble of the Forty-Niners and the California gold mining camps...

By the latter quarter of the 19th century, American dressmakers and designers were going regularly to Paris, to see the latest fashions for the wealthy and well born. When they returned to New York, they set about producing copies, at first for their own exclusive, wealthy clientele and then, later, for department stores and other retailers. For the first time in fashion history, anybody with a buck could buy a Paris designer knock-off, which of course horrified the Paris designers, who jealously guarded their designs from the upstart Americans, just as they jealously guarded the City of Light's position as the world's fashion capital. In 1868, the Parisian designers founded the Chambre Syndicale de la Haute Couture Parisienne to guard their position and prerogatives.

However, even before there was a Hollywood spinning its cinema dreams, popular culture in America and England was competing with uppercrust Paris for fashion cachet, with stage actresses such as Lillie Langtry and Sarah Bernhardt, and the couturiers who dressed them, setting the tone for fashionable women at the turn of the century.

Ms Langtry, for example, a daring Victorian-era British beauty who was said to have had an affair with King Edward VII, and who became a sensation on American stages, had a good instinct for marketing and self-promotion. She parleyed her celebrity as an actress into a second career as a turn-of-the-century celebrity endorser and a prominent advertising figure, promoting products such as Lillie Bustles, Lillie Cream and Lillie Powder.

In any event, it took nothing less than the cataclysm of World War I to cut the golden thread that ran from the Paris ateliers, where the swanky one-of-a-kind fashions were designed, and the New York sweatshops, where the off-the-rack, mass-produced clothes based on those fashions were actually sewn.

World War I meant isolation for Paris couture, just as, a generation later, World War II also did, but it resulted in a flowering for American fashion. In New York, during this period, the very first American designers' fashion show was organised by the editor of *Vogue*.

As the Jazz Age-Prohibition-Depression years between World War I and II blurred by, American designers and fashions became increasingly influential, but expensive and fancy clothes for 'society' still originated in France. By then, Hollywood had its own celebrity designers, such as Adrian, who designed for almost all of the greatest movie stars of Hollywood's first Golden Age, from Greta Garbo and Barbara Stanwyck to Katharine Hepburn and Jean Harlow. American films of the period had a strong fashion influence all around the world, spreading the popularity of everything from the flapper dress and short hair for women to Hawaiian prints and the whole concept of something called 'sportswear', which dated back to the 'rah-rah' fashion-plate Ivy League college boys of the '20s' Jazz Age and their glamorous depictions on film.

Hollywood actors and actresses were fashion trendsetters, whether they aspired to be or not. When leading man Clark Gable didn't wear an undershirt in *It Happened One Night*, the whole undershirt-making industry went into a slump. When it became known that blonde-bombshell Jean Harlow didn't wear underwear under her body-hugging dresses, sexy clothes over simple nudity, rather than over heavy girdles and 'foundations', became a delicious and scandalous American-inspired fashion craze.

During World War II, the City of Light was occupied by the Nazis, which meant that couture, like the rest of life, was promptly 'Aryanised'. American design was again on its own, this time with access to materials severely curtailed because of the pressing needs of the all-out war effort. Silk, for example, was reserved for parachutes, not stockings; leather went for boots, belts and uniforms, not gloves or stylish coats. The restrictions on textiles meant that long skirts and dresses were out; short skirts and boyish jackets, fashion 'looks' that conserved materials, were in. From the front to the factory, Americans in wartime were dashing, and they looked it.

As it has throughout its history, America in World War II benefited from the irrational beliefs and prejudices of its enemies. 'Aryanisation' in occupied Europe meant that artists, scientists and craftspeople in every field who were Jews or who might be other targets of the hate- and prejudice-filled Nazis fled the advancing German armies. From Albert Einstein to playwright Bertolt Brecht, the best and brightest Europeans in every field ran for their lives. Fashion was no exception.

Take for example, the influential designer Pauline Trigere who, for half a century, was associated with New York fashion elegance. Ms Trigere was born in Paris in 1908 to Russian-Jewish immigrants who looked for safety and freedom from pogroms and prejudice in the cosmopolitan City of Light. As a child, Pauline designed her own party dresses and helped out at her father's tailoring shop, according to a fashion-industry obituary. Eventually, she opened a shop with her brother that catered to a smart Parisian set and married a Russian tailor. In 1937, she and her family, which by then included two sons, left her native France for New York, where she taught herself English by going to movies on 42nd Street.

The reason for leaving a successful Parisian life full of future promise? 'Hitler,' Ms Trigere replied. 'Need I say more?'

In America, she was able to start all over again, borrowing from relatives to launch her own wartime clothing line, which led to success after success. Until the war, she said, 'Fashion had to have a European label or it wasn't fashion.' She passed away in Manhattan, after a full and celebrated life, at the age of 93.

In Europe, the end of the war meant the return of the style-setters of Paris couture to their place at the apex of international fashion. In the United States, the end of the war meant the return of millions of young soldiers and the end of all those young jeans-wearing women going off to work in the factories.

The young men and women who had fought and won the war wanted normality and they wanted to settle down and raise families in Levittown or the San Fernando Valley, and in all the other new suburban developments that were then springing up all over the country to house them. Soon, there was even something called the Baby Boom. And all those Baby Boomers, despite their disapproving parents' fears that they were growing up to become savages who didn't appreciate the many sacrifices of the older generation, turned out to like wearing jeans and to be interested in high fashion, too.

Midtown Manhattan in those first post-war days was a glittering, gritty show place, home to the Broadway theatre, at its apex of entertainment influence. It also was the era of influential newspaper gossip columnists, who memorialised the glamorous nightlife and held court in nightclubs with names like Copacabana, Twenty-One and the Latin Quarter. The New York-centred radio industry was about to give birth to the New York-centred television business. Madison Avenue was setting out to conquer the world with unparalleled visions of the Good Life, American-style, which meant big shiny cars, single-family homes and electric appliances. An endless abundance that was the envy of the world.

It was the era of cool in jazz joints like Hickory House, where British-born Marian McPartland played piano in her own trio, and of noir in gritty black-and-white films like *Sweet Smell Of Success*, the 1957 picture starring Burt Lancaster and Tony Curtis.

Success, directed by Ealing Studio veteran Alexander Mackendrick (who also directed the original *The Ladykillers* and *The Man In The White Suit*, among others) anatomised the whole wised-up post-war show-biz/newspaper gossip/emerging-TV scene, with crackling Clifford Odets and Ernest Lehman dialogue and a jazzy Elmer Bernstein musical score.

'I love this dirty town!' declaimed Lancaster, playing powerful, ruthless newspaper columnist 'JJ Hunsecker', who was modelled after Walter Winchell, and whose column could make or break a career or a show. And the line seemed to sum up the feelings of the era.

In the late '40s and early '50s, fashionable garmentos in fedoras and chalk-stripe suits, subwaying in from the Bronx and the other outer boroughs to the Garment District just south of Times Square, could be forgiven for thinking they were working in the very centre of the capital of the world.

In the '50s, the New York Garment District proliferated and specialised, too, with entire Seventh Avenue buildings given over to one specific aspect of the trade – dress manufacturers together in one building, coat manufacturers or even the makers of bridal gowns together in another. The decade brought new man-made fabrics, new media and mass marketing, rapid new modes of international travel; in summary, the whole modern world.

It was a world that Marilyn Monroe, a pouty blonde in a sexy dress, could conquer, just the way that blondes in sexy, revealing, low-cut gowns were conquering the new medium of television (and selling lots of sets to the bedazzled public besides). Celebrity culture and the cult of the red carpet begat the paparazzi and the inevitable shouted question, 'Who are you wearing tonight, dear?'

In 1961, America's stylish young president, who would soon begin his brief affair with Marilyn Monroe, and his glamorous, Sorbonne-educated, French-speaking wife visited Paris. There, it was Jackie, not Jack, who was the sensation. At a state dinner given by French President Charles de Gaulle, the American president introduced himself, famously saying, 'I am the man who accompanied Jacqueline Kennedy to Paris.'

A few months before, during the last month of the 1960 election, the astute publisher of *Women's Wear Daily* had observed wryly: 'Those smart and charming Kennedys – Jacqueline, wife of the Senator, and his mother, Mrs. Joseph P., are running for election on the Paris Couture fashion ticket.'

In the post-Kennedy '60s, in fashion as in music, it was the British Moment, and Carnaby Street, headquarters for influential British designer Mary Quant, was the creative fount for a profusion of miniskirts, bell-bottom pantsuits and vinyl go-go boots.

While Edwardian dandies and colour-coordinated buccaneers stalked the shops on Carnaby Street, The Kinks sang their satirical hit, 'Dedicated Follower Of Fashion', mocking the earnest pretensions of the '60s fashion scene.

Popular music and popular fashion have been fellow

travellers since at least the Gibson Girl. Consider, for example, the latter-day uniforms of disco and grunge – one the height of peacock fashion, the other fashionably anti-fashion, both happily marketed to the kids by Madison Avenue, Hollywood and the fashion industry. Slouching roughly midway between the two, are the Sex Pistols, at the vanguard of British Punk, who elevated tight T-shirts emblazoned with anarchic messages, tight trousers and zippers, safety pins, spikes and chains as accessories, to the status of pop art, and are justly famous for – among other studied outrages – their compellingly discordant rendition of Frank Sinatra's signature tune, 'My Way'.

Punk had its fashion muse, and her name was Vivien Westwood, a young British designer with spiky peroxided hair long before it was a punk fashion statement. Ms Westwood's design innovations include bras worn outside clothing, bare midriffs and corsets. In the early '70s, she opened a small shop with Malcolm McLaren, an art school graduate who later created and managed the Sex Pistols. Their shop had many names and incarnations, including 'Too Fast to Live, Too Young to Die', which was a homage to James Dean and bikers as interpreted by Hollywood B-movies, and 'Sex', which specialised in sado-masochistic gear.

In America, Rudi Gernreich specialised in future shock, too, doing the costumes for *Space: 1999*, for example, the mid-1970s British TV series that starred Martin Landau and Barbara Bain, in their post-*Mission: Impossible* mode. Gernreich introduced see-through dresses, the no-bra look and the 'monokini', a topless bathing suit.

American fashion proliferated, moving right from the high-end department store into the 'trendy' little boutique, and getting all way out to the street, where 'vintage' and second-hand clothes, and even patched jeans, became all the rage. It was a particularly American expression of the old dictum: style leads and fashion follows.

From then on, right through disco, rollerblading, grunge and hip-hop, right up to the present day, 'fashion' was just as likely to bubble up from the street as to be dispensed from on high, by a couturier in a Paris atelier.

The American fashion business, which had developed in the mid-19th century, continued to be dominated by New York City. During the first big waves of immigration from Europe in the 1880s, the Lower East Side teemed with immigrants crowded in tenements and sweatshop factories. 'Couture' may have meant Paris, but ready-to-wear, off-the-rack and mass production all meant New York. And in the 1920s that came to mean Seventh Avenue, the heart of the Garment District in Midtown on the West Side, where, after the creation of the Penn Station railroad hub, the multi-billion-dollar trade came to be centred. It employed more than 400,000 workers at its height in the 1970s, many of them jammed into the six-square block area between Penn Station and Times Square.

By the '70s, the sweatshops still hadn't disappeared, despite three-quarters of a century of union and activist effort to police the industry; though their numbers and their worst excesses were certainly diminished, the sweatshops of yore had simply moved on to where America's latest waves of immigrants were to be found – in particular, to New York's Chinatown and to the suburban sprawl east and south of downtown Los Angeles, where today, for example, the US Labor Department still raids some 200 sweatshops every year. And of course, the sweatshops moved overseas, to the impoverished countries of the developing world, where young and uneducated cutters and sewers might be paid 50c (30p) per hour or even less, compared to the $8 (£5) or more per hour their American counterparts might make.

Today, with American apparel manufacturers at the forefront of the controversial practice of 'outsourcing' the actual assembly of cloth into clothing to countries like Mexico, Thailand and Bangladesh, where the prevailing wages can be just pennies per hour, the New York Garment District still employs more than 100,000 workers, making it second only to LA.

More than two million immigrants arrived in New York City in the first two decades of the 20th century alone, and many of them found their first jobs on the Lower East Side in the rag trade. The American fashion industry's history of immigrant worker exploitation is long and inglorious, and today it also embraces the Mexican and Korean women toiling in Los Angeles sweatshops and the child workers making expensive designer sneakers in Thailand. One criticism of America that rings true, and that Seventh Avenue has exemplified, is this: while there may be no ceiling whatsoever on a poor, but clever and determined (and lucky) immigrant's potential rise to the very pinnacle of life in the United States, it is equally the case that in the present day – unlike many other 'advanced' democracies – there is next to no floor protecting the masses of the poor and their children either. Still, the immigrants keep coming and poor people keep trying. There is that element of truth, and that genius of marketing and publicity, about this aspect, too, of the American Dream.

How many men like Charles Komar and Abe Schrader has the Garment District produced over the decades? In 1908, Kumar, a turn-of-the-century immigrant from Tsarist Russia, opened a small lingerie factory selling high-neck gowns and drawstring bloomers on the Lower East Side. He financed the factory with the $500 he'd borrowed from the Hebrew Free Loan Association. By 1917, Komar & Sons was selling a classic American-made slip, as well as cotton nightgowns and robes.

In those early years, Komar sewed the company's code right onto each piece of apparel he sold. 'We give more to the consumer than either mercantile law or common opinion demand,' the tag read. By the mid-1980s, the founder's 25-year-old grandson was the heir to a $40 million business. In the 21st century the company is still going strong, riding the fashion wave of lingerie's new cachet as outerwear, a style that Vivien Westwood, still colourful and outrageous in her sixties, did so much to promote.

Abe Schrader was Polish-born and -raised, and he might have stayed in his native land for ever if a Cossack pogrom after World War I hadn't sent him fleeing for his life to New York by way of Havana.

Until 1930, young Abe worked in the city's sweatshops, cutting cloth, saving his money, then he opened his own apparel factory on West 38th Street and began making coats and women's dresses. By 1943, Abe Schrader had made his first million dollars, turning out uniforms for the Women's Army Corps. In the post-war years, with Europe in ruins, his coat-and-dress business thrived. Then, in the mid-'50s, inspiration struck.

Air-conditioning was just beginning to spread, and Abe, a sharp-eyed observer of what his customers needed, noticed that women in air-conditioned restaurants tended to keep their jackets on, even when the temperature outside had soared into the '90s. 'So I realized that women needed jackets all year around,' he told *Smithsonian* magazine back in 1985. He started making his dresses with matching jackets, and in the second half of the '50s it became his signature look. Soon Abe's distinctive suits for women were selling in Saks Fifth Avenue and Bergdorf Goodman. By the mid-1980s, Abe Schrader was an octogenarian and, by his own estimation, a 'multimultimultimillionaire'.

The roll call of super-star American designers who rose from humble origins to wealth and worldwide fame includes both Calvin Klein and Ralph Lauren. They both came from the same part of the Bronx, one of the outer boroughs of New York City, that had been the home of Jewish immigrants and their upwardly mobile, middle-class descendants for generations. Lauren was born Ralph Lifshitz and Klein was born Calvin Klein, though back then the name certainly didn't have about it that sexy whisper of cool, that 'it's a Calvin' cachet.

So what's in a name? Would a Lauren by his given name have sold so many preppy clothes?

Lauren founded Polo Fashions in 1968, shrewdly choosing the name because of the 'power, style and intrigue' that its uppercrust and Anglophile associations evoked. The genius of the Lauren formula was to marry the preppy English-tweed look with virile-cowboy Americana. He was the first designer to have his own store and the first to sell a total lifestyle 'image' with all the sophistication and snobbism that implies, and that meant selling home furnishings and accessories along with the clothes.

Unlike Lauren, who was self-taught, Klein developed his flair for fashion and drawing at New York's High School of Art and Design and at Manhattan's Fashion Institute of Technology. He launched his own company in 1968, too, and his first designs were an immediate success. However, what turned him from a successful New York designer into a household name that immediately prompted a frisson of scandalous connotations was his genius for marketing and self-promotion. This became evident after he introduced his trademark jeans in the 1970s with a most titillating and memorable TV and print advertising campaign.

In the ads, photographed by Richard Avedon, Brooke Shields, then a 15-year-old fashion model with a baby face, cooed, 'You know what comes between me and my Calvins? Nothing.'

The ads outraged social conservatives, with TV stations all around the country pressured to decline airing them, but they created a frenzy, with Calvin sales soaring to the unheard-of level of 40,000 pairs per week. In the '80s, Klein added his logo to underwear, both men's and women's, innovating the fashion for women's bikinis that looked like men's briefs. Like Lauren, he expanded into home furnishings, fragrances, accessories and other lifestyle areas.

Boundary-pushing controversy continued to be one hallmark of Klein's advertisements. In recent years he was also accused both of contributing to the fad known as 'heroin chic', using emaciated, stoned-looking models, and of blurring the line between fashion-forwardness and child pornography, with an advertising campaign that featured teenagers in sexually suggestive poses. The publicity and the controversies haven't hurt his business or his cachet with such celebrity clients as Julia Roberts and Gwyneth Paltrow.

The 1970s saw the rise of not only Lauren and Klein, but such other famous names of American fashion as Halston, Diane Von Furstenberg, Gloria Vanderbilt and Donna Karan. But perhaps the singular American fashion triumph of the decade (after HotPants, of course) occurred in France – in the very epicentre of the old royal order, at the Palace of Versailles, where Louis XIV had once held court.

The Versailles Competition of November 1973 pitted French couturiers against their upstart American counterparts. A watershed moment, a turning point in the history of American fashion, a duel of honour between ancient fashion enemies, or simply a very clever publicity stunt? You decide...

Eleanor Lambert was for more than six decades the grande dame of American fashion public relations and her clients included some of New York and Hollywood fashion's biggest names, from Adrian to Oscar de la Renta and Calvin Klein. She knew how to get her clients' ink in the columns and the trades and, perhaps even more importantly, how to enhance her clients' prestige and clout. She was one of the central organisers of the influential New York-based Council of Fashion Designers of America and the force behind the widely noticed annual International Best Dressed List, whose members were selected by a 'secret committee' that met annually at Lambert's apartment.

In the 1970s, she was holidaying in Italy, at the villa owned by Gerald Van der Kamp, then the curator of Versailles, who asked the savvy publicist to think of some way to raise money to restore a royal bedroom in the palace to its former glory.

Hmmm...

A fashion show at Versailles, suggested the publicist – but only if Americans were allowed to participate along with the French, she specified.

'We couldn't do an American fashion show in Paris without looking silly,' the veteran publicist recalled to *Women's Wear Daily* on the occasion of her 100th birthday, in 2003.

The French fashion team included Hubert de Givenchy; Yves Saint Laurent, whose runway shows could be so electric and emotional as to leave the audience drained, cheering and weeping; and Pierre Cardin, a formidable competitor in his own right, an Italian whose name was originally Cardini, and who understood both globalism and ready-to-wear before they were fashionable.

The French demanded that they be allowed to choose the American participants, and the Americans reluctantly agreed, or so the legend goes. On the visiting team were Halston, Oscar de la Renta and Bill Blass (not so incidentally, all Lambert clients), and they competed in a matched pair of high-fashion, high-stakes presentations.

Improbably, the Americans and their presentations triumphed, because of – as *Women's Wear Daily* put it at the time – their 'simplicity and zest'.

'People threw their papers in the air and screamed and yelled. It was wonderful,' Lambert remembered.

And so, by the end of the decade, American designers from the unfashionable Bronx had ascended to the pantheon of international pop-culture celebrities.

Immigrants and the children of immigrants have always made their fortunes on Seventh Avenue, as well as around Ninth and Santee, the downtown Los Angeles equivalent. Only the surnames have changed over the decades. Fashion companies, often founded by these immigrant dreamers, 'sell dreams', says Renzo Rosso, who heads Diesel, the fashionable jeans company based in Italy, whose dreams can cost upwards of $150 a pair. The United States is Diesel's largest market, of course, accounting for 15–18 per cent of the company's global sales of around $0.75 billion. In 2003 those sales financed a 25th anniversary celebration for Diesel in the Veneto, in northeastern Italy just south of the alpine foothills. The celebration featured entertainment by Moby, an appearance by super model Naomi Campbell and an all-day party with a marching band, acrobats, a hot-air balloon, a midget Elvis impersonator and strippers dressed as nuns. It may have been Italy, but it was an all-American celebration of success and excess, an American dream as if choreographed by Federico Fellini...

Formal elegance is another dream that fashion sells. And widespread access to formalwear, once the sole province of society's upper echelon, is another democratising American innovation that started with a single idea at a single, 100-year-old Philadelphia-based company.

Sam Rudofker founded his company, S Rudofker, just after the turn of the 20th century, but it wasn't until his sons took over nearly half a century later that they decided to specialise in formalwear. That's when they came up with the innovation that put a designer tux within the reach of every man:

Tuxedo rentals!

The Rudofker brothers made the tuxedos and sold them to men's stores, and to laundries and tailors with dry-cleaning facilities. A new American business was born, but the newly remade company needed a new name and so, as the story goes, the two brothers spent the day brainstorming with executives at an advertising agency

Nothing stuck. Finally, one Rudofker brother looked down at his watch. 'Let's go home,' he is supposed to have said. 'It's after six.'

After Six?! It became the company's name.

Katharine Hepburn was an on-screen aristocrat who often dressed, both off-screen and on, in tunics and trousers. It was her look and it started an international trend. Audrey Hepburn was an on-screen gamine, unrelated to Kate, and she was best known for wearing capris or a little black dress. It was her look and it also started an international trend.

Hollywood's stars have always been fashion icons, and today's top runway models, who were once simply referred to as living 'mannequins', have become super-model fashion icons and stars in their own right too.

The term 'super model' was popularised in the 1980s, as a category on the original *Star Search*, an American talent-competition TV show, but the idea of the internationally famous model originated in Britain's Swinging Sixties with Jean Shrimpton, the first 'Mod' model, who was followed by Twiggy, a 16-year-old Cockney girl named Lesley, who lived up to her *nom de catwalk*.

By the '90s, famous and wholesome all-American beauties had been joined on the runway by an international cast of so-called 'exotic'-looking (which is to say, non-White, non-Anglo) beauties, including Imam and Naomi Campbell.

Linda Evangelista encapsulated the whole diva ethic of the super model with her famous declaration, 'I don't get out of bed for less than ten thousand a day.' Kate Moss demonstrated fashion's circular logic by personifying the renewed popularity of the waif look, which in our day has again been superseded by what, once upon a time, in the 1950s, preceded it; namely, a curvy bombshell ethos, personified by Brazilian beauty Gisele Bundchen.

Marilyn Monroe would have understood.

When singer-actress Jennifer Lopez wore an emerald-green Versace dress with a startling neckline, plunging right down to her navel, at the 2000 Grammys, the firestorm of publicity hotwired a trend in celebrity skin and daring décolletage, which continues at award shows and premieres to this day. It was another example of the all-American insight that sex sells, and that titillation is just marketing genius, the more synergistic the better.

Ms Lopez, of course, became just one of many celebrities to start her own clothing line. Rappers and hip-hop music moguls, in particular, leveraged their youth appeal with their own branded clothes and accessories. Among the music world celebrities who've tried to turn their fashion sense into big business on Seventh Avenue in recent years are Beyoncé Knowles, Eminem, Eve, Jay-Z, P Diddy, 50 Cent and Gwen Stefani.

So even by the time of New York's Fashion Week in the late summer of 2001 it was just as likely that you would see a rock or movie star on the runway as a professional model, so intermingled had the worlds of fashion, movies and music become. Fashion, just as much as film and popular music, depended on spectacle, on the idea of the 'hot ticket' and the 'fresh new thing'.

Fashion Week, held under great white tents in Manhattan's Bryant Park, adjacent to the vigilant stone lions guarding the massive grey Beaux Art public library on 42nd Street, was a triumph of the publicity and marketing arts. Fashion Week, as it happened, evolved from semi-annual press weeks that centenarian publicist Eleanor Lambert first arranged in 1943 as a way of promoting made-in-America clothes during wartime.

Wartime and fashion collided again, on that sunny, cloudless 11 September morning. Famous designers' staff were already gathering under the billowing Bryant Park tents, sipping morning coffee, unwrapping the new spring lines and waiting for the willowy models to arrive. Ruffles, optimistic colours and bright floral prints were the newest New Thing that week, co-existing on the runway that is fashion's own Yellow Brick Road with Grunge Redux and a fashion fad for camouflage clothes and paramilitary-like gear that some wags had dubbed Terrorist Chic.

Uptown, in the New York Armory on the fashionable East Side, the prestigious Donna Karan show was just setting up.

And then.

At 8:47am, high above the bustling financial centre downtown, the first airliner, American Airlines Flight 11 from Boston, smashed into the North Tower of the World Trade Center at 790kmph (490mph).

Smoke rose into the cerulean sky. All around Manhattan, the sirens began to sound. Under the tents and in the Garment District, a panicky uncertainty flared.

At 9:03am, the second airliner, United Airlines Flight 175, also from Boston, crashed into the South Tower of the World Trade Center.

Within the hour, the Port Authority of New York and New Jersey had closed all bridges and tunnels in New York and the Federal Aviation Administration had, for the first time in history, grounded all air traffic nationwide.

Under the tents, the designers packed up. At the Armory, the National Guard took over from the fashionistas. By early afternoon, its organisers had cancelled New York Fashion Week. Skittish fashion journalists who could, left the city as soon as possible, some in hastily rented cars. It was the end of the fashion world's flirtation with Terrorist Chic.

A week later, on the other side of the Atlantic, London's

Fashion Week went on, but six of the designers cancelled outright, while 61 others carried on, though many cancelled festive after-parties and scaled down or muted the customary extravagances of their shows. Burberry, whose chief executive, a New Yorker, was in Manhattan, cancelled, while at least two other designers dropped out because their models and stylists remained in Manhattan, and didn't know if they could get on international flights.

An industry that had grown dependent on transcontinental travel found itself in lockdown.

A little more than a year later, New York's Fashion Week went on again as planned, though this time with designers showing patriotism and the flag along with the customary skin. Some 13 months after the attacks, employment in the New York apparel industry had begun to tick back up. It was, as ever, good news for the Jews, the Arabs, the Pakistanis, the Chinese, the Koreans, the eastern Europeans and all the other immigrants from all around the world who depended on the sometimes cutthroat mercies of this traditional gateway industry for their first steps up the ladder in American society.

'Manufacturing jobs have done a lot to help New York's immigrants for the last three centuries,' is how New York Democratic Senator Charles Schumer put it at an apparel industry event at the time. 'Those jobs are the ladder up for generation after generation after generation when they come here from all around the globe,' he added. 'All they want is to live a life of dignity...and the fashion industry has provided that.'

'It's been a tough year,' allowed Hillary Clinton, New York's other senator and the former First Lady, who was also there. Then she pointed out that the designer navy suit she was wearing had been made in New York.

Then, inevitably, some time later, designers began to show their autumn 2004 lines. The new emphasis was on romantic, even chaste clothes, and the new 'look' bespoke, not grunge and street smarts, but good grooming and taste. It began to look like fashion could be trying one of its great about-faces.

Critics dubbed it the New Modesty...

6 Courtside At The Garden: The Thrill Of Victory, The Object Lesson Of Defeat

National Basketball Association games will be played in China for the first time this year, and the international arm of ESPN, the American sports network, will televise pro B-ball, the quintessential American sport, in as many as 100 countries next season.

Once, baseball was universally regarded as the undisputed all-American sport, while basketball was generally disparaged by many American television and advertising executives, precisely the sorts of people who wrote the big cheques to big sports leagues, as too 'urban'. But that was simply a delicate way of suggesting that basketball was too inner city, that there were too many very tall Black men on the court, and not enough White faces to attract the great mass audience that supposedly was affected by such things.

Of course, long ago a generation of basketball-mad kids in the suburbs proved all that untrue, and super-humanly gifted athletes like Michael Jordan of the Chicago Bulls and Ervin 'Magic' Johnson of the Los Angeles Lakers demonstrated that skin colour was completely beside the point. And then, thanks to the league's far-sighted commissioner, basketball spread around the world.

Today, America's basketball stars are just as likely to be born in Jamaica or China as Hell's Kitchen, NYC or the Tenderloin, San Francisco and to have names like Vitaly Potapenko, Hidayet Turkoglu, Dikembe Mutombo, Hakeem Olajuwon, Andrei Kirilenko, Manute Bol, Manu Ginóbili and Yao Ming. And it's not just basketball.

Baseball, too, the so-called American 'national pastime', now regularly gets its biggest draws from Japan, Cuba and the Dominican Republic. The biggest stars in golf and tennis, too, the country-club sports so long considered the exclusive preserves of the wealthy White Anglo-Saxon Protestant, are Tiger Woods and the Williams sisters, African-Americans.

Actually, it wasn't until the 1950 season that professional basketball began including African-Americans at all. The first Black player to come out on the court in a Knick uniform was Nat 'Sweetwater' Clifton, one of the three Black pro ball players that year. The other two were Earl Lloyd, who played for the Washington Capitols, and Chuck Cooper, who played for the Boston Celtics.

The old complaints about too many Black players seem ludicrous in these multicultural days. In one sense the TV ratings are the bottom line, and by that measure things have never been better. The viewers are there. When the scrappy Pistons of Detroit took down the mighty Lakers of Los Angeles in the televised fifth game of the finals of the 2003–2004 season, ratings on ABC soared, even sending the stock of its parent company, Walt Disney, up.

Americans are sports crazy. This remains true despite the unending say-it-ain't-so scandals involving multimillionaire sports stars, and despite the seeming best efforts of professional sports team owners to make their fans crazy, or at least drive them away, with high ticket prices and fickle loyalty and extortionate attitudes toward their home cities, which they regularly threaten with the spectre of midnight moves to other municipalities. Such moves will lighten, if not outright eliminate, the team's municipal taxes for decades; and build them their new, state-financed stadiums, with new revenue-generating luxury 'sky boxes' (and those private luxury boxes, inevitably, are the preserves of corporations entertaining clients).

The owners shrug off the criticism and all the appeals to

old-fashioned tradition and fairness, as do the jewellery-bedecked superstar athletes, and their Armani-suited agents, and they all generally respond with something like this:

'Hey, man, fugeddaboutit! It's a free country, ain't it? And after all, pal, getting whatever you can get is the good ol' American way.'

Big-league sport, in fact, may be the ultimate American metaphor. Like the United States itself, the sports world is ostensibly a meritocracy, a Camelot of Individual Excellence and cooperative Team Effort.

Back in the real world, where steroids and scandals and mega-bucks deals dominate the sports pages of tabloid newspapers, and pro players have both rap sheets and super-model girlfriends, there is a dark side to this most American of sandlot and backlot dreams.

Perhaps no game exemplifies this metaphor and these contradictions better than the all-American game of basketball. Contrary to popular opinion, it is, in fact, the only major sport played in the United States that was originated in the United States.

In the 18th century, a recognisable version of a baseball-like game, rounders, was played in England by the children of the Royal Family, and the game's origins go back centuries before that. Football, or at least a game with many of its elements, was played by the ancient Greeks and Romans. Even novelist Jane Austen has a character remark about the game. And in England football was already a rough-and-tumble sport of the roistering lower classes in Chaucer's time. It was transported by the first colonists to the New World.

But basketball was born in Springfield, Massachusetts, in 1891, created by a clergyman who taught at the Young Men's Christian Association and was looking to develop a game that could be played indoors by young Christian men during the long New England winter.

By the turn of the century, basketball was being played widely in colleges on the East coast, and the first semi-professional teams in New England were battling each other, often before boisterous and unruly working-class and immigrant crowds who took great pleasure from watching the speedy American game. From the beginning then, the game created for good young Christian men was popular with the young hellraisers of the street.

By 1915 the Original Celtics, a New York-based professional team featuring tough tenement kids from the Lower East Side, was barnstorming around the country, treating crowds to their original 'meshing' offence, in which players continuously ran figure-eights until the play-making guard, the original so-called 'court general', passed the ball into the teammate best positioned to cut in for an easy basket under the net.

Over the next decade, the game spread to colleges across America, and in 1908 the college game's governing body – the National Collegiate Athletic Association (NCAA) – was created. However, it wasn't until the game arrived at New York's Madison Square Garden in the 1930s that it found its national stage. In 1934 the Garden scheduled its first college basketball doubleheader. In 1936 Hank Luisetti, a Stanford player, happened to shoot the ball one-handed as he leapt into the air in a game with Long Island University at Madison Square Garden. It was the very first jump shot recorded in basketball history and it changed the very nature of the game.

Then in 1938, Madison Square Garden staged the first ever post-season tournament for college teams, which led to the annual NCAA Tournament, the forebearer of today's 'March Madness', and the crowning of a national collegiate basketball champion.

It is no PT Barnum-like exaggeration to call Madison Square Garden the World's Most Famous Arena. Over the years, everyone from Elvis Presley and Madonna to Frank Sinatra and the Pope have played the Garden, home today to the New York Knickerbockers professional basketball team, aka the New York Knicks.

Today's Madison Square Garden, which opened in 1968 at 33rd Street and 8th Avenue, is the fourth arena to bear the name. The first opened in 1879 at 23rd Street and 5th Avenue. It was on the site of an abandoned railroad shed that had been bought and converted to a circus arena by PT Barnum, the 19th-century showman who specialised in bizarre acts (and is famous today for saying that 'there's a sucker born every minute', though, truth to tell, he never actually made the remark).

Barnum himself, a sometime newspaperman from the state of Connecticut, is generally regarded as the progenitor of both the modern museum and the modern three-ring circus. In the 1830s, he was working as a grocer in New York City when he made his fateful detour into showbusiness by 'buying' a woman whom he exhibited to the credulous public as George Washington's 161-year-old 'coloured nurse'. Later, he took her and various other human and other curiosities on the road, among them Chang and Eng, the original 'Siamese Twins', the 63cm (25in) tall 'General Tom Thumb' and a supposed mermaid that was actually a fish to which had been appended a horse's tail.

In 1842, he opened Barnum's American Museum in New York, which specialised in his sideshow oddities; two years later, he took his collection to Europe, appearing before, as he himself ballyhooed, the 'Crowned Heads of Europe', including Queen Victoria.

In 1871, he opened his circus, billing it as 'The Greatest Show On Earth', with such acts as 'Admiral Dot', a midget even smaller than Tom Thumb, and Jumbo the Elephant, a huge pachyderm imported from Britain's Royal Zoological Society.

Today, the descendant of Barnum's original three-ring extravaganza, the Ringling Bros and Barnum & Bailey Circus, still calls itself 'The Greatest Show On Earth' and it still plays the Garden to sell-out audiences every year.

The second Garden opened at the same East Side location in 1890. Arguably, its main claim to fame is that it was on that site, 16 years later, that its famous turn-of-the-century architect, Stanford White, was shot to death by the jealous husband of a girlfriend.

Today, the 76,180sq m (820,000sq ft), 20,000-seater Garden is owned by Cablevision Systems, which, along with ITT Corp, bought the arena for $1 billion in the mid-1990s. Cablevision is the same company that provides cable television service to most of the New York metropolitan area, and it also owns the National Hockey League's New York Rangers and the National Basketball Association's New York Knicks, who debuted at the old Garden in 1946.

In America, as in Europe, it's not usual for a media company, particularly one with major television interests, to buy a professional sports team. In addition to Cablevision, Time Warner, Disney and News Corp all have their own teams. In fact, it's a good example of media business synergy, and, not surprisingly, the show-biz/big-league sports embrace has hastened the proliferation of non-stop entertainment and a host of new distractions to fill every millisecond of time at the stadium during these great modern spectacles, whether the game is basketball, hockey, American football or soccer.

Hockey may be Canadian, but it's become a naturalised citizen of the great state of rabid American fandom. Just ask any New Yorker at the Garden for a Rangers game if the Stanley Cup is not a big part of the US sporting scene.

Hockey is fast, and that appeals to Americans. It's got contact, collisions and sudden, on-ice violence. Americans don't mind that either. But hockey's TV-minded impresarios don't stop there. Even when the sporting action is on hold, the spectators' attentions are engaged by some other activity – a competition for the fans; loud, pulsing music; action replays on big screens, commercials and promotions. And what's true about Canadian hockey and the other big-league American sports has become true about English football too, with soccer importing American-style hype and showmanship into UK sporting arenas.

It's a trend that's going to continue, so look for more neat gizmos, music and flashing lights, and more bouncy girls in skimpy skirts on the sidelines and in the front rows, clapping, dancing and twinkling for the cameras, while the fans roar.

The Knicks play around 41 home games a year in the Garden, and each one sells out, with diehard fans with limited wallets still paying $3,000 for a season pass to a seat high up in the nosebleed section of the bleachers.

For big games, the movers and shakers of the Manhattan business world can be counted on to show up, just as they would for the premiere of a new film or the opening of a hot new club or restaurant. A Knicks game is a scene to seen at, to network at and even to do some business at.

What prominent New York press agent Howard Rubenstein (whose clients have included Donald Trump, George Steinbrenner, Rupert Murdoch and Mike Tyson) said a decade ago is still true today: 'It ain't Le Cirque,' he said, surveying the well-heeled crowd at one packed Knicks game. 'But believe me, it's the hottest scene this town has seen in ages. I can't decide whether to watch the big bodies driving down the court or the well-dressed bodies in the stands.'

Some of those well-dressed bodies in the stands for the Knicks-Toronto Raptors game one March 2003 night at the Garden were wearing Calvin Klein, no doubt, during the deliciously titillating moment when none other than Calvin Klein himself stopped the play with two minutes, 16 seconds left, just as Latrell Sprewell was about to inbound the ball for the New York team.

The famous designer grabbed the basketball star's elbow and whispered something in his ear, while the game halted unexpectedly and the fans courtside buzzed. Then security guards went into action and escorted Klein back to his seat. The next day, the gossip columns were in full-on dish mode. Two weeks later, the designer announced he was going into rehab.

What had he said? The basketball player maintained that Klein had been mumbling and couldn't be understood. But, he added prudently, 'Any type of clothing line, I'm definitely open to, so if Mr Klein wants to do some business, it can be done.'

A year later, it was business as usual for the indefatigable Mister Klein, who could be found one glorious spring morning in Manhattan, underground, with a bevy of super models, trailed by reporters and news cameras.

There he was, patrician-looking Calvin Klein himself, caught up in the morning commuter rush, handing out free $2 MetroCards, as New York subway passes are called, to harried straphangers in various midtown subway stations. It was, needless to say, a promotion, calling attention to his latest line of women's clothing.

Meanwhile, his delay of the Knicks game the previous season had inspired local lawmakers to pass legislation that was promptly dubbed the Calvin Klein Bill, mandating fines of up to $5,000 and/or jail time to anyone who went out unauthorised onto a New York City playing field and delayed a professional sports game.

Famous faces – like film directors Spike Lee (*Do The Right Thing* and *Jungle Fever*, among others) and Woody Allen (*Manhattan*) and actors from Dustin Hoffman (*Rain Man*) to Elijah Wood and Sean Astin (two of the Hobbits in *The Lord Of The Rings* trilogy) – are regularly at court side for Knicks games. And on the other side of the country, actors like Jack Nicholson and Ray Liotta, actor-rappers like Snoop Dogg, directors like Steven Spielberg and actresses like Melanie

Griffith and Dyan Cannon are apt to be court side at Los Angeles Lakers games.

When Sylvester Stallone, for example, turned up court side at a Lakers play-off game, the theme from *Rocky* echoed through the Staples convention centre in downtown LA, where the home games are played, and the crowd gave the muscular actor a standing ovation.

In these days of reality TV, and its evanescent fame and notoriety, even a charismatic loser can become a court-side celebrity. Case in point, Kwame Jackson, the runner-up at the end of the first season of *The Apprentice*, the NBC hit starring New York real-estate magnate Donald Trump. There he was court side at the Garden for a Knicks–Nets play-off game, interviewing Beyoncé Knowles, Jay-Z and Ja Rule for a cable TV sports talk show. After the game, according to the *New York Post*'s Page Six, the standard bearer of the New York tabloid gossip tradition, 'Jackson was mobbed and needed a security escort to walk him out to his chauffeur-driven Mercedes Maybach.'

Said Page Six of the *Apprentice* runner-up, noting archly that the Maybach is a $350,000 car, 'Life is looking good.'

And these days, isn't that the whole point of being an American celebrity?

Not surprisingly, sometimes celebrities are 'comped' into the Garden, just as they are to hot new clubs and restaurants. Celebrities also customarily score pricey 'gift bags', filled with all manner of designer goodies, whenever they show up at an industry or charity event. A bag handed out at a recent event was worth some $35,000, according to organisers. And the presence of celebrities at, say, a televised awards show like the Oscars or the Grammys will have designers, jewellers and top-of-line automobile dealers falling all over each other to 'loan' or outright give away their products. The hope, of course, is that said products or services will be mentioned or seen on TV. But that's another story.

The general theory behind celebrity comping – after all, who can better afford those expensive tickets? – is that their glamorous presence is worth the complimentary court-side seat that would otherwise command £1,600 per game.

Basketball is big business, and nowhere is that more true than in hoops-mad New York. But for the kids who grow up shooting baskets, idolising the stars and buying all their expensive branded merchandise, it's much more than just big business. It's an art, a philosophy, a dream and a way of life. And that, too, is nowhere more true than in New York.

Consider the concrete jungle, the high-rise housing projects with makeshift courts high up on tarry roofs; the kids shooting baskets up there, or playing pick-up games in cracked-concrete outdoor courts in schoolyards, or in tiny pocket parks; dribbling fast and driving toward bent rims without nets. In New York, basketball on the streets is a tough, year-round, all-weather sport.

'Dunk, and people anywhere will ooh and aah,' a New York-bred basketball player once told *Sports Illustrated* magazine, explaining the peculiarities of the Gotham game. 'But you can wow a crowd in New York with ball handling and passing.'

The New York game is 'like jazz, people getting together and just playing', another city-streets player told the magazine. 'It's about choreographed spontaneity.' And it's about finesse, whether it's the kind that head-fakes a bigger opponent or overcomes the obstacles blocking the way from the 'hood to the Dream.

Appropriately enough, the commissioner of the National Basketball Association for the past 20 years has been David Stern, the ambitious but unassuming son of a New York deli owner. The street-smart lawyer took a sport that drew anaemic ratings when it was televised, that was haemorrhaging money for its franchises because it was perceived as too Black, too

New York and too drug-infested, and he turned it into the multibillion-dollar, multifaceted international conglomerate it is today.

He tamed the internecine infighting among the teams' owners and negotiated lucrative broadcasting and merchandising deals for the league, but the key was the salary cap that he pushed through in 1983 and got both the owners and the players' association to accept. That agreement called for the players to get 53 per cent of the gross revenues, including both stadium receipts and broadcast fees, with the owners getting the remaining 47 per cent. The agreement brought both financial stability and labour peace to the game for more than a decade and a half, and gave the players a financial interest in their teams' successes.

Stern also brought a kind of marketing genius to the NBA that it had lacked, positioning the inner-city sport as if it was a latter-day Walt Disney Company, and looking to expand its popularity with both the younger generation and internationally. 'They have theme parks,' he said of Disney more than a decade ago, 'and we have theme parks, only we call them arenas. They have characters – Mickey Mouse, Goofy – [and] our characters are named Magic [Johnson] and Michael [Jordan]. Disney sells apparel, we sell apparel. They make home videos, we make home videos.'

As far back as the late 1980s, Stern went after the kids and pre-teens who would be the next generation of basketball fans by including in a four-year national-broadcast-TV-rights deal the provision that the NBA itself be given a free half-hour of air time for a highlights show that would air right after the network's Saturday morning cartoon and kids' shows line-up. And those cartoon-watching kids just kept on watching when the NBA came on.

Stern also created the climate that internationalised the team rosters of this most American of professional sports. Take, for example, 23-year-old Yao Ming, who is 7ft 5in tall. He travelled from China to Texas in 2002 to join the Houston Rockets. The league's scouts had been aware of him for years, and how could they not be? At the age of nine, he stood 6ft tall. The child of two Chinese basketball players (his mother was on the Chinese women's national team), he played for five years with the Shanghai Sharks, before making the move to the Big Show in the United States.

Former Los Angeles Laker superstar Shaquille O'Neal, probably the best-known player in the sport today, also learned how to play and was discovered outside the United States. Born into a military family, Shaq started playing basketball at an Army base in Wildflecken, Germany, when he was in the sixth grade. There, he once met a college basketball coach, who had come to Germany to conduct a basketball clinic. The coach, making conversation with the young giant he'd found in of all places a military base in the middle of Germany, asked the then 6ft 9in tall O'Neal how long he'd been in the Army.

'I'm just 14,' Shaq replied.

At the time of this writing, one NBA star, Shaq's former teammate Kobe Bryant, is under indictment for rape; another, former New Jersey Nets centre Jayson Williams, has just been acquitted of manslaughter charges. Other NBA players have faced drunk driving or drug charges, or have been involved in bitter, public custody battles.

Not unexpectedly, Commissioner Stern also has made certain that the bad off-court press of some of the league's players, who regularly turn up in the gossip columns living the club life, the drug life or even the thug life, is counteracted by the many good works that the league has undertaken over the years, associating itself with anti-drug and stay-in-school public-service programmes, for example. The NBA also makes certain that its players turn out for charity, such as the 'Miracle On 138th Street' event one recent Christmas season, when such

NBA stars as Jason Kidd, Nick Van Exel, Dikembe Mutombo and a half dozen other marquee names gathered at the Abyssinian Baptist Church in Harlem and helped distribute 150 tons of free food to some 5,000 needy families.

Of course, stay-in-school public-service programmes send one message; youthful teenage superstars who turn pro straight out of high school send another.

Over the years Madison Square Garden has been the site of much more than championship basketball. The arena has hosted everything from political rallies of all stripes to six-day-long bicycle races to wrestling extravaganzas and travelling puppet shows.

In 1932, Franklin Roosevelt accepted his first presidential nomination there, and so, more than four decades later, did Jimmy Carter. In 1957, movie producer Mike Todd and his wife, the actress Elizabeth Taylor, held a party there to celebrate the one-year anniversary of Todd's biggest film, the original *Around The World In 80 Days*, which starred British actor David Niven and Mexican comedian Cantinflas. The original was replete with the requisite star cameos and the cast of thousands, as is the remake, with Jackie Chan taking the Cantinflas comic-sidekick part. In the remake, even the Governor of California does a brief star turn, playing 'Prince Hapi'.

'Cast of thousands' could also describe the televised party at the Garden for the late-'50s original. Refreshments were copious and, by all accounts, were one of the reasons the party descended into such a drunken fiasco, with party guests stealing or destroying the expensive door prizes, including brand-new motorcycles.

In 1962, Marilyn Monroe, sewn into a skin-tight white-silk gown for the occasion, sang her sexy, breathy 'Happy Birthday, Mister President' to President John Kennedy at the Garden.

In 1996, at an altogether tamer affair across town at Radio City Music Hall, President Bill Clinton celebrated his 50th birthday, and was serenaded by the likes of Aretha Franklin, Smokey Robinson, Carly Simon, Kenny Rogers, Jon Bon Jovi and Shania Twain, among others. But this was a different time and a different president, whose 'bimbo eruption' problems were well known, so there was no possibility that there would be a surprise appearance by a Hollywood sexpot in a tight dress to sing suggestively to him.

In 1999, the dress Marilyn wore the night she serenaded President Kennedy, which was encrusted with some 6,000 rhinestone beads and sequins, fetched $1,267,000 on auction in New York.

The dress had become a pricey piece of Americana. It was something Marilyn herself, a bright and sensitive young woman with a manufactured reputation for being a not-so-bright blonde, would have understood. 'An actress is not a machine,' she once said, 'but they treat you like a machine. A money machine.'

In 1971, the Garden was the site of the first of the three memorable Mohammed Ali–Joe Frazier prizefights. At the time, it was an unparalleled American spectacle, a titanic clash with a significance for the watching world of mythic proportions. The young, tall, confident Ali, who'd converted to Islam, returning to the ring after having been stripped of his title for his vocal opposition to the Vietnam War, versus Frazier, a bible-reading fireplug of a hard-charging pugilist, who stylistically and rhetorically was his utter opposite. Both men were undefeated going into the fight.

Ali was a boxer, quick and mobile, who described himself poetically, as The Greatest, who danced like a butterfly, stung like a bee; Frazier was the quintessential hammer-fisted puncher, nothing fancy, but he just kept coming and was said to be unstoppable. In the run-up, Ali repeatedly taunted Frazier as an Uncle Tom, infuriating him and his supporters.

It was billed as the Fight of the Century, and it was the toughest, most expensive ticket in the history of Madison Square Garden to that time. In the crowd that night were Hugh Hefner, Barbra Streisand, Bill Cosby, Dustin Hoffman, Diana Ross and Sammy Davis Jr. No less a personage than actor Burt Lancaster was a colour commentator for a television broadcast, and mega-entertainer Frank Sinatra, the Chairman of the Board himself, was in the front row, working the fight as a photographer, shooting for *Life* magazine.

Ali 'came prancing into the ring in his scarlet robe', the late Alistair Cooke wrote in *The Guardian*. 'He granted the roaring crowd a kind of indulgence, acknowledging their presence by looking down his short adorable nose and lightly nodding his head. He assumed his stool as the heir apparent might await the depositing of the crown by the Archbishop of Canterbury.'

Frazier charged, and Ali slipped aside, batting away his blows. Frazier threw his devastating left hook, and Ali countered with his lightning left jab and left-right combinations. It was a classic match-up, fought at a brutal pace. But Ali also grandstanded, mugging at the front rows during the clinches and, eventually, he was caught by a thunderous Frazier left hook in the last chaotic round. Joe Frazier won a unanimous decision.

Ali 'could have won if he hadn't fooled around,' the third man in the ring, referee Arthur Mercante, recalled to *The Guardian* 30 years after the event, but 'he was more interested in playing to the crowd and throwing pitter-patter punches on the ropes'.

The fight in the Garden set up the two rematches – the Rumble in the Jungle in Zaire in 1974 and The Thrilla in Manila in 1975 – that made boxing history, and Ali won both fights. A quarter of a century after those three monumental matches, the two boxers' adult daughters met in the ring in a New York state casino for a heavily hyped bout, billed as Ali Versus Frazier IV, that was broadcast as a pay-per-view spectacle. The 23-

year-old Laila Ali, a model, beat Jacquelyn Frazier-Lyde, a 39-year-old lawyer, in a decision after the 8-round fight.

The Felix Trinidad–Bernard Hopkins middleweight title fight made boxing-at-the-Garden history of a different sort, when, for the first time ever, some 20,000 fight fans had to pass through metal detectors and submit to a weapons search to get inside the storeyed Midtown arena. The date was 29 September 2001, two-and-a-half weeks after the World Trade Center attacks.

You can be sure that it has not escaped the attention of tall teenagers with superlative hand-eye coordination that sports, and particularly the game of basketball, is a way out of the ghetto, whether that ghetto is in New York City, Akron, Ohio or Ankara, Turkey. That was true when the game was young, when the ghetto was on the Lower East Side and the kids were Irish and Jewish, and it's still true today.

Consider, for example, LeBron James of Akron, Ohio, just 18 years old in 2003, when he signed with the Cleveland Cavaliers. Standing 6ft 8 ins (2m) tall and weighing 110kg (240lb), with good hands, he passed up getting a college education and went pro straight out of Catholic high school. Upon signing, he also got a seven-year, $90 million endorsement contract from Nike, the sports shoe company, as well as a $1 million signing bonus, not from the team, but from Upper Deck, a company that specialises in sports trading cards and other memorabilia.

Of course, LeBron isn't the only athlete and basketball isn't the only game where a charismatic player might make more money from endorsement deals than from playing. Take David Beckham, for example, the internationally known soccer star, whom *Esquire* magazine recently called a 'marketing phenomenon and a gossip bonanza'. As good looking as the young Ali, as shrewd a businessman as Magic and a babe and gossip magnet who is married to Posh Spice, it's no surprise that he's surrounded by a media-savvy team of advisers who are planning his assault on the only territory left on earth that's not yet totally obsessed by professional soccer, and where he's not an instantly recognisable A-list celebrity: America, whose conquest would complete Beckham's Beatles-like celebrity.

In Beckham's case, however, celebrity already pays quite well, thank you very much: Becks and Posh took in £1,000,000 selling photo rights to their 1999 wedding, according to *Esquire* magazine, and his last contract with Manchester United, which eventually traded him to Real Madrid, included a £20,000 per week payment just for his 'image rights'.

An 18 year old turning pro was something new for the NBA, and it was controversial. However, in most other professional sports leagues, teens regularly earn big money on the professional circuit. LeBron was a bad example who will just encourage kids to drop out of school, critics complained. But bad examples about the so-called easy life of the gifted athlete are probably next to nothing as a factor that keeps deserving, but poor kids out of the classroom compared to the sky-high cost of going to college. New York University, for example, now costs $46,000 per year. So for many kids, particularly those with a hip-hop vocabulary and high-top shoes, whether they currently reside in Brooklyn or Bucharest, the story so far of LeBron James sounds just like the American Dream, though of course there are only, roughly, 300 on-court 'jobs', grand total, to be had in all of professional basketball.

Whether or not LeBron will grow into the role that many already have cast him in – the next Michael Jordan, the most beloved and certainly most influential player in the history of the NBA, and, David Beckham not withstanding, still the best-known individual athlete in the world – remains to be seen.

'Air' Jordan, a master of the gravity-defying flying dunk and the balletic fade-away jump shot, won six NBA championships with the Chicago Bulls before he retired. Then he went back for a two-year encore with the Washington Wizards, a low-ranked team in which he also held an equity interest.

In the years immediately after he retired for the first time, television viewing levels for professional basketball overall were off an average two million viewers from when he was playing at his peak with the Bulls – a fall-off that many observers attributed to his absence from the game. When Jordan retired for good in 2003, in a ceremony at his final home game, the United States Secretary of Defense, the controversial Donald Rumsfeld, presented him with a flag that had flown over the Pentagon on the one-year anniversary of September 11.

In his last season with the Bulls, Jordan earned a $36 million salary. Over his entire career, His Airness is estimated to have made more than $425 million from endorsement deals with Nike, Gatorade and the like alone.

That is the dream to which the court-side kids still aspire.

7 Harlem: Home Of The First Black Ex-President And Now A Tourist Magnet For The World

In his eight years in the Oval Office, William Jefferson Clinton presided over a post-Cold War boom time, but he also was pilloried and impeached and nearly driven from office because of his sexual dalliance with a flirtatious young intern from Beverly Hills.

'Lewinsky' became popular slang shorthand for a certain sex act, which, it was said, some among the younger generation didn't consider to be a sex act at all. Seemingly, the President of the United States agreed.

Why did he do it? 'Because I could,' said the 42nd President of the United States, as he made the publicity rounds in the summer of 2004, touting his massive (and massively popular) autobiography. And that was not a good reason, he was always quick to add.

America's sax-playing, shades-wearing, skirt-chasing, popular (and still controversial) ex-Leader of the Free World once was famously described as America's First Black President by Nobel Prize winner Toni Morrison, who explained in a 1998 *New Yorker* essay that he 'displays almost every trope of blackness: single-parent household, born poor, working-class, saxophone-playing, McDonald's-and-junk-food-loving boy from Arkansas'.

When it came time to have his official presidential portrait painted, the one that would join the pictures of Washington, Lincoln and all the others in the White House, he picked a son of sharecroppers for the prestigious task. Painter Simmie Knox became the first African-American to paint a president's official portrait.

Not surprisingly then, since leaving the presidency, Mister Clinton has set up his offices in New York's Harlem, the Black urban ghetto that sprawls across the northern precincts of Manhattan, in a 770sq m (8,300sq ft), 14th-floor penthouse at 55 West 125th Street. He's a fixture there, where, much to the delight of the locals and tourists, he might be glimpsed popping into the nearby Starbucks for an iced tea and then strolling the block or so to his office. He turns up all over New York City, too, maintaining a full schedule of both speech- and scene-making.

'Now I feel like I'm home,' Mister Clinton told a crowd of several thousand on the day in 2001 that he officially moved into his new digs. Then, as *Jet* magazine reported, 'The ex-president sang doo-wop with the Boys Choir of Harlem and embraced several saxophonists as he joined them, singer Chuck Jackson and the crowd in a soulful rendition of "Stand By Me". He was serenaded by songstress Etta James and the gospel group The All Good Singers.'

Rent for the ex-president's Harlem office comes to $345,000 per year, a tab that the federal government picks up. By comparison, the government pays $93,000 per year for ex-President Carter's Atlanta offices, and it paid $285,000 per year for the late President Reagan's Los Angeles offices. The tab for President Clinton in Harlem is just about half of what he would have paid to set up in Midtown Manhattan.

The government also paid around $300,000 more to redecorate the new uptown digs before Mister Clinton moved in. Fittingly, the architect and the designer that the nation's First Ex-Black President chose to do the refurbishing had also recently done some work for rap mogul P Diddy.

Harlem itself is now a regular tourist stop for buses filled with camcorder-carrying White people, tourists from Scandinavia and elsewhere, who want to partake of the sublime uplift that a testifyin' gospel church service can provide, or just get some authentic down-home fried catfish fingers, crispy fried chicken and waffles perhaps, or maybe some collard greens and ribs. Sunday service at the Abyssinian Baptist Church, followed by a bus tour, a gospel show and an authentic soul-food brunch at the Cotton Club, all for just $75. Or for just $25 more to do Harlem at night, with stops along the way in the fancier Harlem neighbourhoods, such as historic Sugar Hill, with drop-ins at jazz clubs and local restaurants. How did that happen? Why did idiomatic Black American cultural flowerings, from jazz to hip-hop (and yes, there are tours for fans of hip-hop, too), find such avid followers in Europe, Japan and elsewhere throughout the world? And what are the historical roots of this latest Harlem Renaissance?

There is the Harlem of the imagination and there is the Harlem that is bisected by 125th Street, today also known as Doctor Martin Luther King Junior Boulevard, an area of north Manhattan that for much of the past century has been regarded as the Black Mecca.

Harlem's modern history begins with the Great Migration of southern Negroes to the cities of the North that accompanied World War I, when wartime defence plants didn't care so much about the skin colour of able-bodied workers. But the history of Harlem goes back much further than that.

In a wooded Harlem park the tulip tree still stands under which, according to famous local legend, Peter Minuit 'bought' Manhattan from the Indians for the Dutch West India Company in 1626. That transaction with the Indians, probably the Lenape tribe, who had no concept of property rights, was supposedly for a handful of trinkets and a few guilders, worth about $24 (£15), and it instituted almost four decades of Dutch rule.

But the district was originally named in 1658 by Peter Stuyvesant, the peg-legged former soldier who was then the Governor of New Amsterdam, as New York was called between 1626 and 1664, which is when the British took it over.

Stuyvesant called the northern part of the island of Manhattan 'Nieuw Harlem' after the Dutch city of Harlem, as the story goes, and despite the change in colonial administration the area kept the name.

For the next 200 years, Harlem was farm country, an area of country estates for the gentry of lower Manhattan, including such prominent early families as the Beekmans, the Bleekers, the Delanceys and the Rikers (all now prominent place names in modern New York). Then, in the 1880s, the elevated railroad reached Harlem and, for the next quarter of a century, Harlem was fashionable (and White), home to an opera house and a yacht club, among other amenities.

The elevated railroads and the extension of the New York subway system to 145th Street in Harlem fuelled a real-estate and construction boom in the late 19th century. Blocks of row houses, tenements and fashionable luxury high-rise apartments with the latest in modern amenities – namely, lifts – went up all over Harlem.

But then, in 1904, the real estate bubble imploded, leaving block after block of newly built apartment buildings without tenants. A Black-owned real-estate company, Afro-American Realty Company, began buying up commercial properties at deflated bargain prices and renting them to the then-emerging Black middle class who, like other struggling American ethnic and racial groups, wanted nothing more than their own homes on nice, safe tree-lined streets.

Within a few years, Harlem had become home to new, majority-Black, 'nice' residential neighbourhoods, such as elegant and exclusive Sugar Hill, the home for Harlem's civic and cultural leaders. Sugar Hill's very name signified all the sweetness that then could be bought by anyone with the money to afford it.

But in many parts of central Harlem, which Sugar Hill overlooked, the real-estate collapse persisted right up until

World War I and the Great Migration to the North. At the time, anti-Black prejudice in New York, as elsewhere, was rampant (in 1905, for example, a pygmy from the Belgian Congo was exhibited for several weeks in a cage inside the primate house of the Bronx Zoo). But financial considerations trumped even racist 'principles', and Harlem's cash-poor White landlords opened their vacant buildings to any Blacks who could pay rent. Blacks from the South, from the Caribbean and elsewhere poured in.

In approximately a decade and a half, Harlem's population quadrupled. Central Harlem became what it has been ever since: a majority Black neighbourhood.

First America and then, soon after, Europe. Everywhere everybody was dancing to a jazz music beat. And the progenitors and the proselytisers of jazz, like Louis 'Satchmo' Armstrong and Jelly Roll Morton, were, of course, Black.

In the Jazz Age, during the 1920s, the artistic flowering in Harlem put its mark on the entire country. Harlem was home to the writers Langston Hughes and Zora Neale Hurston, the sculptor Augusta Savage and such musicians as Louis Armstrong, Duke Ellington and Bessie Smith among many, many others.

For White people with money, the centre of fashionability in New York moved north, to Harlem, and to such legendary nightspots as the Cotton Club, the Savoy Ballroom and the Apollo Theater. Of course, to some degree it was simply patronising rich White people revelling in the 'exotic' and the so-called 'primitive', and it was as much about seeking out forbidden thrills in Harlem's gin mills and bawdy houses as it was about an appreciation for sophisticated entertainment that crossed ethnic and socio-economic boundaries.

But it was also undeniably an 'expression of cultural nationalism involving the dynamic circulation of ideas among a biracial group of urban artists, critics, and activists', as Christopher Dunn, assistant professor of Spanish and Portuguese and of African–American diaspora studies at Tulane University, put it in the journal *Black Renaissance/Renaissance Noire*.

While the performers and entertainers of the Harlem Renaissance catered, to some unfortunate but necessary degree, to the hackneyed expectations of their White audiences for minstrelsy, they also were subverting those very stereotypes with bravura displays of their originality and genuine mastery. And talent was something that the very best artists on the other, paler side of the Colour Line understood.

Some Jazz Age Americans travelling in Europe even scandalised the supposedly sophisticated locals Over There. 'The whole of Venice is up in arms against Cole Porter because of his jazz and his Negroes,' Boris Kochno, ballet impresario Serge Diaghilev's private secretary, complained to a friend in 1923. 'They are teaching the Charleston on the Lido Beach! It's dreadful!'

The Renaissance in Harlem lasted as long as the good times did. Then, in 1929, the stock market crashed, and the good times disappeared along with the money. Where once had been lines of fashionably attired swells waiting to get into the Cotton Club, to listen to sophisticated jazz and sip cocktails, now there were breadlines of 'forgotten men'. Unemployment in Harlem soared to 50 per cent.

What had been a Black enclave, an oasis, now became regarded as a Black ghetto, a dangerous, desperate zone. The glamour of the nightlife gave way to the perils of the mean streets. And hard economic times in Harlem were relieved only because the slide toward World War II meant that, once again, the needs of the defence industries and the military pushed aside the clichés of racism. Nonetheless, in the war itself, young Black soldiers fought in segregated units in a segregated Army, and it was only after the war that the United States Army was integrated by President Truman's executive order.

In the post-war '50s, returning soldiers and veterans of the defence plants began to press for equality and their share of the same American Dream for which, they had been told, everyone was fighting.

One of the many unforeseen consequences of the Great Migration was that a new secular, multi-racial audience was exposed to the sanctified southern spirituals and the gospel music of the Black churches. The same was true of the traditional folk blues sung by southern sharecroppers, prisoners on chain gangs and others in the vast southern Black underclass, and that music began to sound on northern streets and in northern factories, too. The unemployed millions in the Great Depression, regardless of colour, were learning a thing or two about the blues themselves. And that appreciative audience – White, Black, immigrant and native born – just grew and grew in the years leading up to World War II.

World War II was a fault line shaking across all of popular culture, and across the wider society too. Kids going off to fight needed their good times, too, and it didn't hurt to remind them that the cute bobbysoxer who liked to swing dance was part of what they were fighting for. But generally, afterward, in the post-World War II years, the millions of returned soldiers and all their kids were surrounded by an influential 'official' pop culture of bland bromides and idealised platitudes. In the first two decades of television, for example, there were hardly any non-White faces to be seen, nor were many social issues raised in prime time on the small screen. In movies, as on TV, self-censorship, in the form of industry-imposed Codes, held sway. But there was an exuberant parallel efflorescence of 'unofficial' pop culture – of be-bop, of new forms of 'cool' jazz, of spoken poetry, of rhythm 'n' blues and of rock 'n' roll.

It was music from the streets, not from the academy. Like today's rap and hip-hop, all of these forms, but particularly be-bop (one of hip-hop's most direct progenitors), were feared and derided as 'race music' by the guardians of the mainstream pop cultural canon. But that did little to hurt their popularity, especially among the kids.

By the late-'50s, the ecstatic gospel music of southern Pentecostal and other Black churches had long been widely appropriated for distinctly secular purposes, in tunes sometimes written by Whites but sung mostly by Blacks. Consider 'Saved', written by the songwriting team of Jerry Leiber and Mike Stoller. Though White, Leiber and Stoller wrote numerous hits for Black rhythm 'n' blues singers, including Big Mama Thornton, The Coasters and The Drifters. Their 'Saved' was an exuberant 1961 R&B hit for LaVern Baker. In it she sang: 'I used to smoke, drink and dance the hoochy-coo, but now I'm SAVED... People let me tell you about Kingdom Come... I used to cuss, fuss, and boogie all night long, but now I'm SAVED.'

It sounded like the same kind of down-home testifyin' that had been attracting the poor and downtrodden of both races to revival meetings for decades, but it wasn't gospel music. It was a sexy, mocking satire and it became a cross-over dance hit.

Meanwhile, during the period of the inclusive Civil Rights crusade of the mid-'50s and the early '60s, progressive Whites linked arms with determined Blacks in street marches, sang 'We Shall Overcome', and pressed ahead with sometimes perilous joint mass actions to protest state-sanctioned inequality and to register new voters in the segregated cities of the South.

In August 1963, more than 200,000 Americans gathered in front of the Lincoln Memorial in Washington to listen, transfixed, as Martin Luther King Junior proclaimed, in the traditional cadences of the southern preacher, 'I have a dream!'

A national Voting Rights Act passed Congress in 1965. But almost at the same moment of that epochal victory, the brief progressive and populist era was being jostled aside by the military misadventure in Vietnam, and by rising anger at the daily oppressions of persistent, though unsanctioned, racism.

The era of Blacks and Whites, progressive American Jews prominent among them, together at the barricades gave way in the cities of the North before Black Power, Black Pride and Black nationalism, and a renewed emphasis on Afrocentrism. The Black Arts Movement of the period specifically rejected the White academy and its traditions, while championing 'street' language and 'performance' poetry.

In 1965, Watts, a sprawling Black ghetto in Los Angeles, exploded in riots, looting and chaos. That same year, Malcolm X wrote his autobiography with journalist Alex Haley (*Roots*), the dramatic story of his rise from poverty and prison that eventually became the basis for a Spike Lee film starring Denzel Washington.

In popular mass culture in the 1960s, TV's lily-white sitcom families from the '50s were finally joined by a dashing team of integrated espionage agents in *I Spy*, a one-hour action-adventure drama. In it, Bill Cosby played 'Alexander Scott', a Rhodes scholar who was also a covert CIA agent, and Robert Culp was 'Kelly Robinson', his professional-tennis-playing partner. The show was significant in the history of television on a couple of counts – not only for the two characters' utter equality, which was taken as a given, even though Cosby's character was obviously the brains of the duo, but also because it was the first series in the history of American television to film extensively on location all around the world, from Mexico to Hong Kong, using an innovative portable studio that the show's cinematographer created especially for it. It became the model for many future on-location shoots.

As the 1960s wore on, Vietnam and the battles in America's streets made an integrated team of spies for the CIA seem more than just a little problematic as role models, and the series went off the air after the 1968 season, which was arguably the most politically and culturally fraught year of the whole tumultuous era.

The wholesome Black–White duo of *I Spy* was followed in the late '60s and '70s by a cycle of low-budget 'blaxploitation' B-movies, in which the villain was inevitably The Man and the hero might be a pimp (as in, for example, *The Mack*, 1973, a blaxploitation cult classic). Of course, back then mainstream commercial culture wasn't quite as adept at adapting to and exploiting 'fringe' and 'counter' cultural themes as it has become since. The blaxploitation movies of the late 1960s and early 1970s, including *Cooley High*, *Black Caesar* and *Cotton Comes To Harlem*, have been repackaged by one Hollywood studio as the 40-title Soul Cinema collection. The studio, MGM, has also licensed a line of retro clothes based on the blaxploitation films' more outrageously kitschy period costumes.

Harlem in the 1970s blaxploitation era was widely seen as inhospitable and dangerous to outsiders with white skin, particularly after the inner-city riots that swept American cities in 1967 and 1968. In the '70s Harlem remained mired in ghetto poverty as its neighbourhoods continued to deteriorate, and in the '80s the plague of crack cocaine spread its misery there, as well as through the other inner cities of America, eventually reaching out to the suburbs too.

In the mid-'70s, during a period when American rock 'n' roll was generally regarded as bland and coopted – and 'outrageous' meant Parliament or Funkadelic – a new authentic voice began to emerge, first from the streets of Harlem and the New York boroughs of Queens and the Bronx, expressing the frustrations and the anger, as well as the aspirations, of ghetto kids.

It had a distinctive beat, it had its own way of dressing and its own language drawn from the argot of the ghetto street: '40 Deuce' was 42nd Street, around Times Square, in New York, for example; and '40 Dog' was a 40oz (1.2 litre) bottle of Olde English 800 malt liquor. 'Ay yo trip', 'bag up' and 'phat' were the kind of words and phrases that flavoured a typical conversation. The New Thing spat back at the conventional hopes of the conventionally upwardly mobile, with its gritty, syncopated, crotch-grabbing, backwards-cap-wearing, fist-in-your-face-waving celebration of authenticity and street credibility. It spat back with its sex, drugs and violence. With its bling-bling-bedecked gangstas. And with its talk of bitches and niggaz, of pimps and ho's.

Parents hated it. Authority figures and civic leaders hated it. Sensitive souls were appalled by it. Bill Cosby to this day hates it. Even Spike Lee decries it. But the kids, even pink-cheeked, baby-faced kids in the leafy suburbs, a world away from the grim realities of the 'hood, loved it.

Hip-hop. Rap. Gangsta rap. Ay yo!

Broadly speaking, of course, hip-hip is more than just the music, it's the culture, and it includes rap, deejaying and emceeing, sampling and scratching, breaking, graffiti art, spoken-word poetry and performance.

Rap's roots run broad and deep, tapping into African traditions, southern Black American traditions and '60s Jamaican pop and reggae. And its influences include the 'emcees' in seventies New York clubs, a decade later, rhymin' 'n' rappin' over the boogie-down dance music they were playing.

Rap's sources also include 'a cappella and doo-wop groups, ring games, skip-rope rhymes, prison and Army songs, toasts, signifying and the dozens, all the way back to the griots of Nigeria and Gambia', as rap record-company owner Paul Winley put it in David Toop's well-regarded history *Rap Attack 2: African Rap To Global Hip Hop*. ('Toasts', 'signifying' and 'playing the dozens' are all derived from ancient African oral traditions. Playing the dozens, for example, is a duelling form of ritualised verbal insult, widespread from the ghetto street to the suburban grade school, of the 'Your mama's so fat that...' form. 'Griots' are traditional West African singers of folk tales and histories.)

One of rap's founding deejays was Clive Campbell, better known to rap history as Kool DJ Herc, a Jamaican who made his way to the Bronx in New York. Kool DJ Herc is generally credited with innovating the idea of break music, or scratch, that dancers in clubs found so irresistible. He was the first to use two turntables and two copies of the same record to play the same hot section of a record, or 'break', over and over, cross-fading between the two turntables. Eventually, he began adding other fragments of music and sounds to create the recognisable hip-hop collage.

Rap's poetic precursors were there in the early '70s, too, in the Los Angeles-based Watts Prophets, who recorded *Rappin' Black In A White World* in 1971; in The Last Poets, who recorded their first, self-titled album in 1970, following it with *This Is Madness*, and in Gil Scott-Heron, whose influential jazz-backed sung poetry included such songs as 'The Revolution Will Not Be Televised' and 'Whitey On The Moon'. They all were political, oriented toward Black Power, and they all recorded fierce and articulate political diatribes to jazz beats.

Rap and hip-hop didn't start out celebrating the gangsta style or painting angry word pictures about bleak life in the ghetto. The first rap hit to make radio's Top 40 (and thereby to catch the attention of suburban, White fans) was Sugar Hill Gang's 'Rapper's Delight' in 1979. It was danceable bubble gum music with a driving bass line, from a Jersey music label with a Harlem name, and with burbling lyrics in pop's great tradition of hummable blather:

I said a hip hop the hippie to the hippie
the hip hip hop, a you don't stop
the rock it to the bang bang boogie say up jumped the boogie
to the rhythm of the boogie, the beat
skiddlee beebop a we rock a scoobie doo

and guess what America we love you
cause ya rock and ya roll with so much soul
you could rock till you're a hundred and one years old

By 1982, two years after Black Entertainment Television was founded and one year after MTV: Music Television first went on the air, rap's ambition had turned darker and edgier.

In 'The Message', Grandmaster Flash painted a memorable portrait of life on the mean streets:

I can't take the smell, I can't take the noise
Got no money to move out, I guess I got no choice
Rats in the front room, roaches in the back
Junkie's in the alley with a baseball bat
I tried to get away, but I couldn't get far
Cause the man with the tow-truck repossessed my car

'Don't push me,' the chorus warned, 'cause I'm close to the edge... It makes me wonder how I keep from going under.'

It was political, it was in what quickly came to be known as the gangsta style, and you didn't have to search out 'alternative' or 'urban' radio to hear it. It too became a crossover hit.

Mark down Her Majesty, the Queen of England, as one of the early fans of the various expressions of hip-hop. In 1983, the Roxy Tour, one of hip-hop's earliest international expeditions, toured Europe, playing for the Queen. The Tour featured, among others, Afrika Bambaataa ('Planet Rock'), the Bronx-born creator of electro funk, who added Kraftwerk samples to the beat, and is generally regarded as the first to call the new style 'hip-hop'; Fab Five Freddy, the Bed-Stuy, Brooklyn-born rapper and actor, who first made a name for himself as a graffiti artist; and the break dervishes of the Rock Steady Crew, one of the best-known break-dancing B-boy groups of the period.

One likes to imagine Her Majesty in private, after being treated to those energetic and expert displays of the B-boys flipping, dropping and spinning, catching some of the vapours herself, windmilling and getting down.

Then in 1985, rap had another huge crossover hit in 'Walk This Way', a collaboration between Run-DMC and Aerosmith, and MTV, accused in its early years of focusing exclusively on music made by White musicians, gave the integrated hip-hop video heavy air play.

From the beginning, MTV was about more than the music. It was about clever marketing of music industry 'product' with video clips that were, in the words of one of its cynical early producers, all about 'smoke machines and chicks', and that was something that hip-hop video producers understood from the get-go. And from the beginning hip-hop videos, reflecting the themes of the music, revelled in booty and bling-bling.

Interestingly enough, one of the other early videos featuring rap artists to receive heavy rotation on MTV was 'Sun City', a 1986 protest against the racist policy of apartheid in South Africa at the time. That recording, featuring some of the biggest musical stars of the period, including Bob Dylan, Miles Davis, Bruce Springsteen, Jimmy Cliff and Run-DMC, was organised by Springsteen's E Street Band mate, Steven 'Little Steven' Van Zandt.

Today, Van Zandt is better known for playing 'Silvio Dante', the owner of the Bada Bing strip club and one of the New Jersey mob family's inner circle on HBO's influential hit crime saga, *The Sopranos*.

In 1988, 'Yo! MTV Raps' debuted on the cable network, bringing hip-hop into suburban American cable homes. The original host of the show was none other than Fab Five Freddy himself. By the late '80s, MTV had also gone international, and it took with it hip-hop. Also at the end of that decade, the Grammys gave its first award in the hip-hop category. Taking note of the fact that the musical genre had been around for at least a decade before the Grammys noticed, MTV's older-skewing sister network, VH1, is in 2004 handing out for the first time what it calls 'the Hip-Hop Honors' in a TV special that will salute the pioneers of the genre.

Today, Russell Simmons is hip-hop's premiere impresario and arguably its most successful entrepreneur. In the mid-'70s, he was just another middle-class Black kid from Queens, who – despite enrolling in City College, and despite the best efforts of his college-educated parents – was drifting into the seductive thug life of drug dealing, flashy clothes and petty crime. However, his younger brother, Joey, known as 'Run' in the clubs, was right in the middle of the new thing, 'rapping' in a group called Run-DMC, and Simmons soon became the group's manager.

One group led to another, managing led to promoting and, eventually, the creation of a hip-hop label. Simmons and Rick Rubin, another college student and the co-founder, called the label Def Jam. Simmons then dropped out of school.

Russell, Joey, the other two members of Run-DMC (Darryl McDaniels, or DMC, and Jason Mizell, or Jam Master Jay) and the rest of the Def Jam acts took hip-hop on the road. By the mid-'80s hip-hop was on fire in the culture and Def Jam had a distribution deal with Sony. Run-DMC itself had an early hit with 'It's Like That', and then became colossal after 'Walk This Way', the collaboration with Aerosmith. It was the first hip-hop group to break totally through to the mainstream – their unlaced trainers and baggy jeans became not only an urban uniform, but the look of kids everywhere – and the first to be featured on the cover of *Rolling Stone*.

In 1999, Simmons sold Def Jam to Universal Music for $120 million. Today, the successor company, Island Def Jam, does some $700 million in sales annually.

Def Comedy Jam and Def Poetry Jam, both on HBO, made Simmons an award-winning TV producer. And when he took it to Broadway, Def Poetry Jam, part of the Spoken Word Movement, which is essentially rap without the bass-heavy musical backing track, won a Tony in 2003. Simmons has launched successful magazines and successful film franchises (*The Nutty Professor*), and he markets a soda (DefCon3), a debit card (Rush Visa) and a signature mobile phone (from Motorola), among other products.

Today, Russell Simmons lives on a $14 million, eleven-bedroom estate in the woodsy suburbs of northern New Jersey. Among the antiques and the extravagances is a sign in the foyer: 'Waiting Room for Colored People'.

Simmons also founded Phat Farm, a fashion company that in 2002 made an estimated $29 million in profits on $263 million in wholesale sales. Phat Farm markets itself as 'classic American flava with a twist', and the word 'phat' itself has made it into the newest editions of the dictionary.

Phat's line of ghetto-chic clothes can be found at most suburban malls, and White teenage boys in the 'burbs are the line's biggest customers. In fact, hip-hop clothes are so mainstream now that, for the most part, they're just stylish clothes that school kids of all colours and backgrounds wear. Gone for many parents and kids are the original negative connotations, gone are the despairing observations that accompanied the style's earlier years, with critics taking the baggy look as being synonymous with the gang look, saying that the baggy silhouette was intended to make the wearer a more amorphous target for drive-by shooters from rival gangs.

Now, marketers estimate that so-called 'urban wear' is a $2 billion per year business, and that fully one out of every four 'discretionary' dollars spent in the country today is 'influenced by hip-hop', according to *Business Week* magazine.

In 2004, Simmons sold Phat Fashions for $140 million to the St Louis-based clothing manufacturer, the Kellwood Company.

Simmons is married to Kimora Lee Simmons, a former fashion model, famous on the catwalk since her early teens, who regularly turns up in Page Six and other gossip columns, in items that often breathlessly celebrate her conspicuous consumption and her 'diva-licious' behaviour.

Kimora, who also designs for Simmons's Baby Phat line, recently bid $16,000 at a New York charity event for the honour of having Manolo Blahnik, the shoe designer celebrated in *Sex And The City*, name a new shoe after her. She was outbid by a New York podiatric surgeon, who paid $20,000. Now that's phat.

A background of violence and of animosity to and by the police is one too common feature of the rap life. In 2000, for example, Gil Scott-Heron was arrested in New York for possession of just over one gram of cocaine and two crack pipes, and he spent ten days in jail. At the time, he argued that he was a victim of racial profiling. But the next summer he pleaded guilty to possession of a controlled substance, agreeing to a plea deal that called for 18–24 months of inpatient drug rehabilitation. The start of rehab was postponed, however, until after Scott-Heron completed a European music tour.

Even rappers with a solidly middle-class background seem to run afoul of the law, and it does their images with the CD-buying public no harm at all, though the rappers will usually tell you the cause of their difficulties is racism. Consider rapper Sean 'P Diddy' Combs, formerly 'Puff Daddy' Combs, of Mount Vernon, New York.

Mount Vernon, by the way, is a planned community in Westchester County, just north of the New York City borough of the Bronx, that was created more than a century and a half ago for working-class New Yorkers and others of high 'moral character, industrious habits and the desire to promote a common purpose' by becoming Mount Vernon property owners, as the small, majority-African American city's official history puts it.

Originally, Sean moved with his mother from Harlem to Mount Vernon at the age of two, after the murder of his father. P Diddy's closest competitor for the title of most famous Mount Vernonite is probably the actor Denzel Washington.

Combs left Mount Vernon to attend Howard University in Washington DC, but it was a New York music-industry internship that led to his career as, first, the wunderkind A&R man responsible for the careers of Jodeci and Mary J Blige, producing their albums in what became known as 'hip-hop soul' style. Then he became a recording artist in his own right.

In 1993, P Diddy formed his label, Bad Boy Records, and his first breakout star was Notorious BIG, whose debut album was the prophetically titled *Ready To Die*. In 1997, Sean Combs released his own first solo album, *No Way Out*, which went on to win the Grammy for Best Rap Album of the year.

In the late '90s, Puff Daddy, as the stylish young music mogul was then called, had his own run-in with the police, when he was accused of assaulting a rival record executive. The original charges were assault and possession of a deadly weapon. That was reduced to second-degree harassment, and the punishment was a one-day anger management class.

In 2000, Combs made tabloid headlines again when he was charged with firing a gun in a crowded nightclub and then fleeing with his entourage, which at the time included his girlfriend, the singer-actress Jennifer Lopez. After a high-profile trial, he was acquitted. Subsequently, Puff Daddy announced that henceforth he would be known as P Diddy.

Today, he remains the head of Bad Boy Records. He is also a well-reviewed movie actor (*Monster's Ball*) and a successful fashion designer, as well as a fixture in the gossip and society columns.

P Diddy's five-year-old Sean John Clothing line sold some $300 million worth of clothing at retail in 2003, and is currently available at more than two thousand stores. In autumn 2004, he's scheduled to open his own first retail store, on Manhattan's Fifth Avenue; earlier in the year, former girlfriend J Lo's own first retail store opened in an upscale mall in fashionable, but faraway, Moscow, Russia.

Ms Lopez herself was scheduled to travel to the Moscow store's opening, and do the honours personally, but instead, on the very day the store was to open, she 'secretly' married singer Marc Anthony instead, exciting and surprising the gossip columnists, and unleashing a torrent of other publicity besides, including the breathless tidbit that had British bookmakers already taking bets against the nuptials lasting more than one year.

The Russian businessman licensing J Lo in Moscow was said to be furious, too. But in newly capitalist Russia, Ms Lopez was in little danger of ending up in the Gulag, though she might find herself in a courtroom, contesting a breach-of-contract suit.

Lately, Sean Combs has confounded professional celebrity watchers, who often expect nothing better than shallowness and bad behaviour from famous rappers, by running the 42km (26 mile) New York Marathon and making his Broadway debut, in a revival of *Raisin In The Sun*. He played the role made famous by Sidney Poitier in 1959. Combs also surprised even some of the cynical when he turned up unannounced – but not without camera crews – at a local classroom in the hip Chelsea area of Manhattan, to take questions from kids whose teacher had assigned the play, by the late playwright Lorraine Hansberry.

Also in that production of *Raisin*, for which P Diddy himself received the expected 'mixed' reviews, is Phylicia Rashad, of *The Cosby Show* fame. At the 2004 Tonys, Ms Rashad won a Tony for best leading actress in a play, becoming the first African-American woman to win Broadway's biggest prize.

'When I was little my mother taught me I could do anything and I wouldn't be scarred by racism,' Ms Rashad said afterward. 'This is an honor for any actress and that's the truth.'

Is rap essentially antisocial, 'mad-dogging' conventional society? Does it undo the hard-won social progress of the past half century by putting forward 'niggaz' and 'thugz' as ghetto ideals, precisely the kinds of stereotypes that were once at the very heart of prejudice against African-Americans? Does rap reflexively demean women and celebrate the thug life?

Or does rap speak to kids from hard-scrabble urban reality and strike a universal chord?

Does the hardcore gangsta attitude of many of the most popular rappers reflect simple reality or does it create it? Is rap 'authentic' or has it just been manufactured by cynical big corporations looking to reach disaffected kids in the suburbs with the 'authentic' sounds the kids in the inner cities like?

The debate on these questions has been raging since the first 'Yo, dawg!' rang out on stage. John H McWhorter, a right-of-centre scholar and the author of *Losing The Race: Self-Sabotage In Black America*, put the anti-rap argument this way in a recent essay: 'Many writers and thinkers see a kind of informed political engagement, even a revolutionary potential, in rap and hip-hop. They couldn't be more wrong. By reinforcing the stereotypes that long hindered blacks, and by teaching young blacks that a thuggish adversarial stance is the properly "authentic" response to a presumptively racist society, rap retards black success.'

'Tip Drill', a recent Nelly video, is one example of what Mister McWhorter and others find so objectionable. In it, huff offended critics, the rapper swipes a credit card between a Black woman's buttocks! Be that as it may, what the unexpurgated video does plainly show are many beautiful young Black women in thong bikinis, shaking their bottoms and their bosoms, while the rapper and others leer and point at their booty, and throw greenbacks at them.

'Put yore ass up, mama, put that dip in yore back,' raps Nelly, to images, electronically smudged, of naked breasts and buttocks, and of naked women embracing suggestively in the shower. 'It must be yore ass 'cause it ain't yore face,' he continues, genially patting a bare bent-over bottom. Interestingly enough, 'Tip Drill' is not untypical of what might be called the booty-poppin', or wiggle-it, genre of rap video.

It may not even be the most blatant. Other videos of the day feature equally scantily clad young dancers and equally suggestive poses, and also include simulated S&M and fellatio. It is, at the very least, a long way from 'American Bandstand' or even 'Soul Train'.

Nonetheless, the particular 'demeaning' sexual imagery in the Nelly video set off something of a furore at one prominent Black women's college. With a 'Tip Drill' student protest planned, Nelly abruptly cancelled an appearance at a charity event at the college, Spelman, in Atlanta, Georgia.

'Black entertainers have become the new myth makers, showing gangsters and bikini-clad women with hyperactive libidos,' Zenobia Hikes, vice-president for student affairs at Spelman College, told the Associated Press. 'For non-black children it creates a gross misrepresentation of the black experience.'

On the other hand, rap's gritty world view is simply part of the 'rhetoric of resistance', as it was characterised in a recent article by Baruti N Kopano, co-director of the Black Studies Program at Delaware State University, in a *Western Journal Of Black Studies* essay, and it can be traced back to the 'coded' speech and musical traditions of enslaved Africans in the United States and elsewhere.

'Rap as a music form employs some of the same elements found in African American spirituals, blues, gospel, jazz (especially be-bop), and R & B,' Kopano wrote. 'Some of these elements include call-and-response, word creativity (punning), hyperbole, spontaneity (freestylin'), and braggadocio... These are some of the same characteristics found in Black speech and in Black literature.'

In this view, if rap is misogynistic, profane and violent, well then, so is the larger society, and rap is simply one more expression of it.

After all, when an African-American entrepreneur recently announced that he was forming an exclusive New York social club, to be called the Harlem Club, for prominent African-American and Latino businessmen, he declared that rappers, athletes and the rest of the 'ghetto fabulous crowd' need not apply. However, the $5,000 charter-member fee would be waived for female 'associate' members, he added, but they had to submit a photograph and meet rigid standards: no older than 35, college educated, childless and unmarried, fit and not overweight. In summary, female associate members of the Harlem Club were required to be babes.

To the criticism that generally took the tack that he was setting up a 'meat market' for wealthy African-Americans, the entrepreneur, who is married, replied that his wife 'takes her butt to the gym, and she keeps it tight for me. I want it all, and I got it all. There are men who want the same.' Women, too, so it seems. The club was deluged with applications from accomplished, ambitious knockouts.

Sometimes, hip-hop credibility came dearly, and sometimes rappers even paid the ultimate price. By the mid-'90s, two of the most talented figures in the hip-hop world – Tupac Shakur and the Notorious BIG – had been murdered in drive-by shootings.

Shakur was killed in a hail of bullets on a street in Las Vegas near the Strip after leaving the Mike Tyson–Bruce Seldon heavyweight championship fight. BIG was gunned down a few months later, leaving an industry party in LA after the Soul Train Music Awards.

Gang war between the Bloods and the Crips, two powerful Los Angeles-based gangs, was one theory.

Bicoastal gang war in the rap world itself, between LA's Death Row Records, headed by Marion 'Suge' (pronounced as in 'Sugar') Knight, and New York's Bad Boy Entertainment, headed by Puff Daddy Combs, was the related theory, which posited that each of the music companies was associated with one of the rival LA gangs. But to this day, neither murder has been solved.

Neither has the seemingly senseless murder of Jam Master Jay, deejay for Run-DMC, a group never associated with gangs or gangsta violence, been solved; to the contrary, its members always condemned rap's glorification of the gangsta lifestyle. Jam Master Jay, a beloved figure in his neighbourhood (partly because, unlike many other rappers, he didn't move away), was shot dead in the band's recording studio in Queens, New York.

Part of rapper 50 Cent's credibility stems from the fact that he's been shot nine times. Despite the multiple charges of possessing child pornography and of having sex with an under-age girl, rapper R Kelly's popularity remains undiminished. Rapper Lil' Kim, famous as much for her revealing costumes as for 'Lady Marmalade', has been charged with perjury arising from her grand-jury testimony about a shootout between members of her entourage and a rival rapper's outside a New York radio station in 2001; she's pleaded innocent and trial date has been set. Even White rapper Eminem went to court and was fined after pulling a gun on rivals. Rappers Ice-T and Snoop Dogg both claim to have been pimps before starting their music and acting careers. And Rapper Ja Rule, 50 Cent's bitter rival, has neighbours of his Inc Studios (formerly Murder, Inc) in the fashionable SoHo section of Lower Manhattan up in arms because of the constant late-night party noise, according to Page

Six, the *New York Post*'s widely read gossip column. Yet another rapper, TI, enhanced his street credibility by secretly making an unauthorised music video while doing time in a Georgia jail.

Rapper Jay-Z is one of many top-of-the-charts rappers who once dealt drugs, including, in his case, crack. But that was then, and this now. Jay-Z heads Roc-a-Fella Enterprises, which includes not only music and clothing, but a brand of vodka, too. As his partner, Damon Dash, told *Business Week* magazine, 'People exploit us, and we exploit them back. If they're going to make a buck off us, we'll make a buck off them. That's just the way it's going to be.'

It may sound crass, and it is, but it's a prudent stance for anyone with an eye to Black history, including the history of Black roots music. Consider this:

Alan Lomax is justly famous as the northern White folklorist of the 1930s who took recording equipment to collect the traditional songs and rhythms of the rural South, and thereby preserved an African-American blues tradition that might otherwise have been lost. It was he and his father, also a folklorist, who discovered Leadbelly, Muddy Waters, Memphis Slim and Sun House, among many others. He brought their music (and, in some cases, them) to a wide, multi-racial audience and in many cases arranged to have their songs published.

But.

According to David Hajdu, the author of *Positively 4th Street: The Lives And Times Of Joan Baez, Bob Dylan, Mimi Baez Farina, And Richard Farina*, Lomax also arranged to have his name listed as co-author on more than a hundred of those songs, including 'Rock Island Line', 'Good Night, Irene' and 'Tom Dooley', so that he and his heirs could collect royalties.

Is it any wonder that even many successful Blacks look at America a 'little bit different', as comedian-actor Chris Rock once put it? 'You gotta look at America like the uncle who paid for you to go to college,' he said, 'but molested you.'

Not all uncles take unwelcome liberties, of course. Tim Duffy, a young White man from Connecticut, for example, is a latter-day folklorist who has dedicated his life to helping the remaining living blues pioneers, who are now old and sometimes frail, and in need of everything from a quick cash infusion to help pay next month's rent or buy medicines, to help getting to their next gig. He, too, has recorded scores of unknown old-time blues pioneers – Etta Baker, Little Freddie King, Haskel 'Whistling Britches' Thompson, 'Captain' Luke Mayer, to name just a few – through his non-profit Music Maker Foundation. In fact, in the past decade Duffy and his wife have made 50 CDs of authentic blues, recording many of the approximately 100 roots musicians that the Foundation helps. And the musicians get 100 per cent of the profits.

Rap music today doesn't only sell music and anti-social attitudes; in fact, it sells almost everything, from beer to cars to the latest fashions and the biggest Hollywood films. Hip-hop novels are even the freshest new thing in the American publishing business, where the genre has been dubbed Gangsta Lit. Is it any wonder that there are now, according to one estimate, more than a hundred hip-hop millionaires?

Russell Simmons and P Diddy are hardly the only hip-hop entrepreneurs to diversify their product lines. Nelly, to cite just one of scores of possible examples, lent his name in 2003 to an energy drink called 'Pimp Juice', which was also the title of one of his songs. Of course, there were immediate calls for a boycott, by, among other groups, the National Black Anti-Defamation League, objecting to the stereotype. But the negative publicity was still free publicity, and it still drew attention to the new drink.

According to one hip-hop news report, Nelly struck deals with two big music-store chains to stock the drink. Pimp Juice sold over a million units in just three months, according to the report, making it the hottest new seller in the energy drink category.

So ubiquitous has rap become as a soundtrack for Madison Avenue advertisements aimed at younger, hipper, more urban-minded consumers that hip-hop entrepreneurs like Russell Simmons are also engaged as highly paid consultants of cool by blue-chip, Fortune 500 companies. Most big Madison Avenue advertising conglomerates also own at least one boutique 'multicultural' speciality agency, too.

Camrys, Corollas, Accords and Civics all have separate African-American-themed advertising campaigns. So do beer brands, quick-service restaurants, department stores, beauty products and on and on. Still, as Blacks and Latinos in the advertising world will themselves be the first to point out, the percentage of advertising dollars spent reaching minorities still doesn't match their growing percentage of the American population. But those dollar totals are growing, and advertising-dependent American media are paying attention.

The reason for the new notice is as simple as the numbers from the US Census Bureau that show that in the first three years of the millennium, while the overall American populace grew by 3 per cent, the Hispanic population surged by 13 per cent, to almost 40 million, more than one-third of whom are under the age of 18. Asians increased by more than 12 per cent and African-Americans grew by 4 per cent to 37 million people. While Whites, who increased by just one per cent in the period, make up 197 million of the 291 million Americans, and 15 per cent of them are over 65. So, inescapably, the country is getting browner, and that part of it which is is also getting dramatically younger.

Media companies read these numbers and they commence to courting these minority communities as never before. For example, in New York, WCBS, a major network-owned station, now celebrates Black History Month with 'The Sounds of Harlem', a special that was shot at the historic Lenox Lounge and is intended to show viewers 'how many of today's biggest pop stars are influenced by legends such as William "Smokey" Robinson, Lena Horne, Harry Belafonte, Miles Davis and the first lady of song, Ella Fitzgerald', as the station's publicity puts it.

One arts- and culture-oriented cable network, Trio, commissioned a documentary called *The N-Word*, which examined that fraught racial term, looking at its origins, its evolution and social significance, its appearances in hip-hop and comedy routines and its metamorphosis from the most dire of derogatory terms into a common expression in youth culture today. Appearing in interviews in the documentary were George Carlin, Ice Cube, Whoopi Goldberg, Samuel L Jackson, Damon Dash and Russell Simmons, among others.

A recent television advertisement for Pontiac's Vibe sports wagon begins with a club disc jockey heading out of his comfortably cluttered apartment to his car, filled with his deejaying equipment – and beautiful young women stylishly dressed for a night on the town. The ad cuts to the crowded club dance floor, with the deejay now spinning records for sexy dancers. 'Find your Vibe', is the tagline. The TV ad, like many focusing on the African-American market, associates the product with sexiness, style and cool, all to a hip-hop beat and, like virtually every other TV ad it aimed at younger, hipper people, it employs the MTV music-video sensibility of quick cuts and snippets of music.

So mainstream have rap and hip-hop become that they now rate their own American television network. Gospel music, for that matter, is getting a dedicated cable network, too. At this point, both the hip-hop and the gospel networks are in advanced development. Hip-hop also has now produced enough oldies-but-goodies and great moments in history so that it even rates its own museum – the Hip-Hop Hall of Fame Museum is scheduled to open in autumn 2004 in – where else? New York.

Perhaps it is time for a museum. After all, the influence of rap and hip-hop worldwide now extends to such disparate mainstream musical icons as The Beatles and flamenco. In Los Angeles recently, a deejay and hip-hop producer who goes by the nom de rap of Danger Mouse created a sensation when he took the vocals from Jay-Z's *The Black Album* and remixed them over samples from The Beatles' *The White Album*, creating the unauthorised but widely disseminated (through online file-sharing, of course) *The Grey Album*. Meanwhile, half a world away, in Spain, a new thing called 'Flamenco Fusion', mixing hip-hop and rap with Spain's traditional folk music, has purists there outraged and the kids dancing. Then again, presumably other purists were put off in the '50s by Miles Davis and his flamenco-infused *Sketches Of Spain*, too.

To the kids around the world who talk Black and dress Black and listen to urban music, obviously rap is more than simply a Black thing. The international success of Detroit rapper Eminem, for example, a small, skinny White kid who grew up in a Black neighbourhood, demonstrates – if such demonstration is required – that rap's specifically Black roots have universal relevance, that it's as much about class and economic background, and about sensibility, as it is ethnicity and race.

Alienation and deprivation, rage and hopelessness strike chords, not just in the victims of discrimination, but in those teenagers and young people of whatever colour who see themselves as being put upon and victimised by the entire misconstruing adult world. Those same younger people generally have a healthy interest in all things sexual and most things crass, just as they always have had. All around the world, younger audiences are watching the reality-show genre, for example, often the very same shows they're watching in the UK and America, just tweaked for the locals.

Today's teenagers may be 'trying on' a lifestyle and a culture, as well as its attitudes – as an earlier generation of would-be suburban rebels and outlaws tried on hippie clothes and attitudes – and for many of them it may be no more than a safe form of teenage rebellion. But it surely doesn't seem like a phase to the kids and young adults presumably passing through it.

And like it or not, rap and hip-hip have been incorporated into the mainstream in the usual ways, via Madison Avenue and Hollywood. The British poet laureate, Andrew Motion, even delivered a birthday rap to Prince William, and Polish break dancers, of all oxymoronic improbabilities, have even spun and flipped in the Vatican for the Pope.

The process of cultural blending itself is all-American – as all-American as, say, a cult samurai-movie double feature on a Saturday afternoon. After all, didn't the stylised samurai movies of post-World War II Japan draw heavily on the traditions and conventions of the American cowboy movie, particularly on the grand-scale Westerns made by director John Ford, movies like *Red River* and *She Wore A Yellow Ribbon*? And then weren't those samurai movies transformed back again in the '70s, into the so-called Spaghetti Westerns, some of the best of which were directed by Sergio Leone, movies like *Once Upon A Time In The West* and *The Good, The Bad And The Ugly*, starring all-American cinema icons like Henry Fonda and Clint Eastwood? And isn't it all being transformed yet again in such densely referential epics of cross-cultural fusion as Quentin Tarantino's two-part *Kill Bill*?

8   From Purple Sage And Blazing Guns To Black-Top Highways And The Neon City: Good Guys, Bad Guys And The Rise Of Rebel Chic

The American media elite, jetting between LA and New York, may disparage the great expanse of land between the two coasts as 'flyover country' – from 12,200m (40,000ft) up, the endless chequerboard of fields is a vision of agricultural bounty and bucolic small town America. But the American heartland is not merely the world's breadbasket; it's also the rich soil from which America's ur-myth of the loner and the lone range rider grew.

Nurtured by the full-blooded adventurers who roamed the Great Plains, the western mountains and the Great Southwestern Desert, the myth came to encompass the romance of the rebel and the outlaw biker. It's been the stuff of storytellers since before Hollywood's earliest days.

But the heartland is more than just quaint and retro. Great cities dot the vast interior landscape, too:

• Chicago, broad-shouldered, mercantile, the centre of a Black artistic and cultural renaissance in the 1930s and 1940s, with a skyline like something out of a 1930s science-fiction movie, unmatched anywhere in the United States, except by the spires of Gotham;
• Detroit – Motor City – home not only of Fords and Chevys, but of The Supremes, The Four Tops and The Temptations; all the signature groups of Motown, a signature American sound;
• Minneapolis and St Paul, the Twin Cities of the northern plain, bisected by a great river, hardy and civilised capitals of a historic liberal tradition;

• Milwaukee, Wisconsin home of that all-American symbol of chromed power and black-top independence, the Harley-Davidson motorcycle;
• Dallas, Texas, the city that oil built;
• New Orleans, the cosmopolitan bouillabaisse at the mouth of the meandering Mississippi River;
• Kansas City and St Louis, in the heart of the heartland, great cities rising out of the great plains, important both to the great Westward Expansion and to the history of the indigenous American music called jazz.

It's a country the size of a continent, after all. It's the land of new starts. You can lose yourself, or find yourself, somewhere, here.

Why do people everywhere love the United States? You can say it in a single word, one that kids everywhere, in whatever language, can understand. It's simple, pardner, it's...

The Cowboy.

That steely-eyed, square-jawed, straight-shootin', all-American cowboy, riding alone, living by his wits, his skills, his code and his speed with a six-shooter. He's polite to ladies, but it's his horse that's his true friend. Yup.

Picture him the way the world does, in his chaps and boots, his ten-gallon hat and low-slung six-shooters, gazing out with that clear, eagle look. Consider the Myth of the Cowboy, the myth the whole world knows. Here are some of the words that conjure that myth: rugged, brave, often solitary: Living a rambling life on the trail... Sometimes raucous, rough and rowdy, sometimes untamed and romantic... An excellent horseman... Living by traditional values of responsibility and sacrifice... Confident, with a quiet faith that one lone, skilful and persistent man can triumph... Rough and tough and instinctively noble... The Marlboro Man.

Of course, there's the cowboy of beloved imagination and traditional Hollywood creation, and then there's the real thing.

The real first cowboy in America – the hard, steely-eyed range rider, herding longhorn cattle on epic drives across vast plains – was...

A Mexican vaquero.

In Spanish, the word *vaca* means 'cow', and the word *vaquero* literally means 'cowman'. The vaqueros first crossed the Rio Grande heading north some two decades before the Pilgrims landed at Plymouth Rock.

The hard-riding, steely-eyed, range-riding vaqueros were usually lower-class mestizos (that is, part Spanish and part Indian); while their employers, the criollos, were usually lighter-skinned and higher-class Spanish-born landowners of New Spain, as Mexico was then known. They were the noble 'Dons' and 'Grandees', who expanded their vast land holdings northward from Old Mexico to the new land-grant territories of New Mexico, into Texas and California and throughout what eventually became the American West.

Years before the Pilgrims celebrated the first Thanksgiving, one of the wealthiest of the early criollas sponsored an expedition that took thousands of sheep and cattle to the open grazing lands and free range of northern and western greater New Mexico.

As far back as the first years of the 17th century, the mestizo vaqueros were driving the free-ranging Spanish cattle for the criollos, back from the northern territories or from the plains of Texas to Mexico City.

Many traditional cowboy terms and practices – familiar from a century of Hollywood movies – are Spanish and derive from the era of the vaqueros. They include words like 'wrangler, chaps, and lariat' and practices like the 'round-up, branding, the western saddle, roping, and [cowboy] clothing', according to a National Park Service history of the period.

In 1821, a revolution freed Mexico from Spanish rule. That same year, the first Americans arrived in Texas, and traders blazed the Santa Fe Trail between Independence, Missouri, and distant Santa Fe. That new trail opened up a reliable route for trade and emigration between the United States, which since the Louisiana Purchase of 1803 had held title to the non-Spanish lands stretching all the way to the Pacific Ocean and the Pacific Northwest, and the vast lands of the Southwest, including both California and Texas, that were then in Mexican hands.

In 1836, 22-year-old Samuel Colt perfected a revolving pistol, and a decade later his Connecticut company began manufacturing the Colt six-shooter, putting a new level of lethal firepower in the lone range rider's hand. In 1846, on what is now generally regarded as a pretext, the United States declared war on Mexico, and by the next year, American military forces under the command of General Winfield Scott entered Mexico City. In 1848, with United States Marines posted at the very 'Halls of Montezuma', Mexico signed the Treaty of Guadalupe, ceding Texas, New Mexico and California to the Americans. A year after that, construction on the first railroad line west of the Mississippi River began.

The era of American expansion across the Far West was underway. It was the era of cowboys and outlaws; of Pony Express riders and stagecoaches; of Conestoga wagon trains winding along dusty trails through hostile Indian territory; of Army forts and lawless frontier settlements; of lone-star sheriffs and bawdy saloons. In short, it was the era that gave rise to all the tropes of Hollywood Westerns.

The true cowboys of Hollywood myth and American history roamed the Wild West in the second half of the 19th century. The real cowboys weren't necessarily Anglo and they weren't necessarily White.

Bill Pickett, for example, was a real working cowboy in the last quarter of the 19th century. Eventually, he turned from riding the range to the sport of rodeo, where he became the premiere exponent of 'bulldogging', that is, the practice of throwing steers to the ground by grabbing their horns and heads. Pickett was an African-American, the first to be inducted into the National Cowboy Hall of Fame in Oklahoma City, Oklahoma.

Typically, the real cowboys drove herds of longhorn cattle from Texas north to the railheads on the great plains, tough cow towns with names like Abilene and Dodge City. Generally, the real cowboys were hardened Civil War veterans, who went West after being discharged, according to the National Park Service history, and sometimes wore their old military uniforms, which were 'adapted to face the elements. Chaps were worn over pants to protect the cowboy's legs while riding, boots to the knee to keep out gravel, spurs to urge the horse to move quickly, bandanas to keep dust from their faces, and hats to protect their heads from the heat and rain.'

The true era of the cattle-driving American cowboy was brief, lasting only some two decades, until the late 1880s, when barbed-wire fences had closed off the West's vast tracts of free range and the railroads had extended their tracks southward to where the great cattle herds grazed.

Decades before the first Hollywood film depicted heroic cowboys, Europeans knew of them and their exploits through bombastic 'dime' novels and from travelling wild west shows, of which William 'Buffalo Bill' Cody's was by far the most famous.

Many of those thrilling dime novels were written by the prolific Edward Zane Carroll Judson, better known by his pseudonym of Ned Buntline, who wrote more than 400 tales of Wild West derring-do. In fact, it was dime-novelist Buntline himself who convinced the colourful range rider who went by the name of Buffalo Bill to act in his play, *The Scouts Of The Plains*. And that was how Buffalo Bill began his long and successful showbusiness career.

Buffalo Bill's show, billed as 'The Best Show on Earth', began touring the United States and Europe in the 1880s, and it continued on the road well into the first decade of the 20th century. Cody himself was a former Pony Express rider, a former scout for the US Army and a former buffalo hunter, who claimed to have killed more than 4,000 of the great beasts that once freely roamed the western plains. As a hunter, he had a good eye; as a showman, he had the instinct for self-promotion of someone born for the limelight.

Billed in Europe as 'Nature's Nobleman', he headed a travelling troupe with as many as 500 performers, including sharpshooter Annie Oakley and the Indian chief Sitting Bull, who had been the principal chief of the Sioux nation when Lieutenant Colonel George Armstrong Custer and some 200 soldiers under his command were killed in the Battle of Little Big Horn.

The Buffalo Bill Wild West Show's rodeo-style performances often included displays of sharp shooting, trick riding and fancy roping, and elaborate recreations of famous Indian–cavalry battles, of course including the Battle of Little Big Horn, with Sitting Bull himself among the actors. The Indians typically were depicted as bloodthirsty savages attacking innocent 'settlers', who then were saved, in the nick of time, by Buffalo Bill and his men thundering to the rescue.

Long before Hollywood, Ned Buntline and Buffalo Bill fixed the image of the heroic cowboy, battling savage Indians and rescuing fair maidens, in the public's mind.

Cowboys were real, so were lawmen and outlaws. Wyatt Earp, Doctor John Henry 'Doc' Holliday and William Bartholomew 'Bat' Masterson were real historical figures; so were the outlaws Jesse James and William 'Billy the Kid' Bonney. Time and again, Hollywood has depicted their lives and mythologised their stories. But naturally, Hollywood made up a lot of stories and characters, too – take, for example, the many on-screen adventures of the 'singing' cowboy, Gene Autry.

Autry, the Lone Ranger, Hopalong Cassidy and Roy Rogers, to name just a few Hollywood Golden Age cowboys, were figments of writers' and directors' imaginations, but were no less influential or heroic to generations of children all around the world for being so.

The first Hollywood cowboy movie star was Gilbert M Anderson, born Max Aronson, who was better known to silent movie fans as *Bronco Billy*, and the first feature-length epic Western of the silent film era was *The Covered Wagon*, made in 1923, well within the lifetimes of some of those who had actually settled the West.

The Covered Wagon appropriated many of the conventions of the wild west show genre and put them on the screen for the first time: the threatened wagons circling, the whooping Indians attacking, the ride to the rescue and, of course, the happy ending in which the Indians and the dastardly villains alike were vanquished. The stagy acting styles of some of the actors in the movie look badly dated to modern eyes, but at the time audiences around the world were thrilled by the film's authentic period look, the long lines of actual Conestoga wagons, the actual Indians on horseback and the grand Western vistas, filmed in glorious black and white.

Other early cowboy stars of the silent period included William S Hart, whose flashing good looks practically defined the early-era term 'matinee idol', and whose characters tended to have names like 'Yukon Ed', 'Bad Buck Peters' and ' "Silent" Texas Smith', and Tom Mix, the so-called 'King of the Cowboys', who started out in the wild west shows and graduated to silent films in which he did his own stunts, and whose characters, when they weren't called 'Tex' or 'Buck', were invariably named 'Tom'.

Although many of the early cowboy stars, even those born in New York City, learned to ride and rope on the Western range, and made their living performing in rodeos or wild west shows, perhaps the most authentic of the screen cowboys was Tim McCoy, who was born in Michigan but went West as a young man after seeing the Buffalo Bill Wild West Show and meeting Buffalo Bill himself. Eventually, he found ranch work in Wyoming.

Interestingly enough, Wyoming, which had long been associated with the cowboy ethic and didn't become a state until 1890, was the first territory in the United States to grant women the vote, enacting a universal suffrage law in 1869, even before the completion of the transcontinental railroad.

In his time in Wyoming, McCoy not only learned to ride, rope and sharp shoot, but he picked up the language of the local Arapahoe Indians and learned their traditions and ways. When World War I came, he enlisted and rose to the rank of colonel; after the war, he returned to Wyoming and became an Adjutant General and a Territorial Indian Agent. That was when he was found by Jesse Lasky, head of the Famous Players production company and the producer of *The Covered Wagon*, who asked McCoy to provide real Indians as extras for the epic.

In 1924, a year after Tim McCoy headed to Hollywood with a band of Arapahoes, tough, independent-minded Wyoming became the first state in the union to elect a female governor.

McCoy became a technical adviser on the film and from there moved into acting, signing a contract with the Metro-Goldwyn-Mayer studio in Culver City, California, to act for the then magnificent sum of $300 (£190) per week. In his first picture, *The Thundering Herd* (1925), he was credited as 'Colonel TJ McCoy'. In his movies thereafter, he was just plain Tim McCoy. In World War II, he again joined up and fought in Europe. Unlike many other silent stars, who fell on hard times after the dawn of talkies and died in poverty and obscurity, McCoy left the movies while still a big box-office draw, toured for a period in his own wild west show, hosted a children's TV show in Los Angeles in the early 1950s and became a well-to-do rancher, living into the late 1970s.

When he won a local Emmy for his TV show in 1952, McCoy, who was up against another children's show called *Webster Webfoot*, wasn't there to claim the statuette, reputedly having exclaimed, 'I'll be damned if I'm going to sit there and get beaten by a talking duck!'

The Hindi-speaking cinema of Bollywood isn't the only one to combine melodramatic action, romance, comedy and song, in a generally unrealistic but entertaining way. No sooner had movies begun to talk in the early 1930s than Hollywood trotted out the singing cowboy, a staple of the thousands of B-movie Westerns that Hollywood turned out in the first decades of the sound era.

'B-movies', often formulaic Westerns, comedies or gangster pictures, were the low-budget bottom halves of double features, and they were shown all around the world.

The most famous singing cowboy was, of course, Gene Autry. His movies in the '30s and '40s, and his early '50s TV show, were genial fables for children, replete with yodelling and bluegrass music, homespun homilies, and, of course, Champion, the Singing Cowboy's splendid sorrel stallion (actually several similar sorrels played the part over the course of Autry's career), who was billed as The Wonder Horse of the West. Typically, Champion received higher billing than even Gene's leading ladies.

In his nearly 100 B-movie Westerns, Gene Autry almost always played himself, though he was sometimes billed as 'Ranger Gene Autry' or 'Sheriff Gene Autry'. The movies were often set in some fantasy version of the 'modern' Old West of the '30s and '40s, with characters not only riding on horseback, but also in jeeps and cars, even flying in airplanes, and using phones and radios. Typical film titles were *Saddle Pals*, *Riders In The Sky* and *Melody Ranch*, which also was the name of Autry's radio show.

Autry, a successful songwriter whose titles included 'Back In The Saddle Again' and 'Here Comes Santa Claus', and who also recorded the Christmas classic 'Rudolph The Red Nosed Reindeer', even promulgated his own Cowboy Code (for example, 'The Cowboy must never shoot first, hit a smaller man, or take unfair advantage' and 'He must keep himself clean in thought, speech, action, and personal habits'), and he used his movie wealth shrewdly, buying TV and radio stations and a major-league southern California baseball team.

But Autry wasn't the first singing cowboy. Ken Maynard, an expert rodeo and Buffalo Bill Wild West Show trick rider, who gave Autry his start in films, was. In the late 1920s and mid-1930s he was wildly popular, making $10,000 a week for pictures like *Mystery Mountain* and *In Old Santa Fe*. But by the mid-1940s, the once-dashing and fearless film actor's weight had ballooned, and he was making just a fraction of that for bit parts in B-pictures. Soon, his film career was over.

He went back to performing in the rodeos, but, sadly, died an alcoholic, alone and impoverished.

By the early 1930s, movies were talking, and as soon they had learned to make noise the sounds of gunfire, war whoops and stampeding hoofs were heard in bijous all around the world. The advent of sound meant the end of the careers of some of the best-known screen cowboys, whose voices or acting styles weren't suited to the new cinema, but one silent-film actor went on to become the personification of the American cowboy.

If he'd wanted a career in politics, he could easily have been the first actor to become president of the United States, so beloved and emblematic of America did he become. But that honour went to a lesser action movie star. The Hollywood actor who did become president of the United States, the late Ronald Reagan, called him 'more than an actor; he was a force around which films were made'.

John 'Duke' Wayne was born Marion Michael Morrison in Winterset, Iowa, and went on to college at the University of Southern California in Los Angeles, where he was on the football team. While at USC, he took a summer job as a low-level prop man on a Tom Mix movie, where he was discovered on the set by director John Ford, for whom he eventually made a series of memorable Westerns, beginning with *Stagecoach*, the 1939 movie that made him a star. In the movie, set in spectacular Monument Valley, he played the role of the 'Ringo Kid', the brave and noble young cowpoke who befriends a prostitute and saves the stagecoach and its passengers from the menacing Geronimo and his band of marauding Apaches.

During World War II, Wayne starred in a series of war movies (*The Fighting Seebees, Back To Bataan, They Were Expendable, Sands Of Iwo Jima* and others) that raised him from a star of the first rank to the very incarnation of the American military man, fighting fearlessly against evil and for right.

Their names suggested what kind of military men his characters were: 'Wedge' Donovan in *Seebees*, Colonel Madden in *Bataan*, Lieutenant Ryan in *Expendable*, Sergeant Stryker in *Iwo Jima*.

For generations of movie-goers around the world his manner in his movies personified the ideal American man. There was always thunder in his fist, even as there was an appealing hint of a friendly drawl in his voice and often a genial twinkle in his eye. But there was nothing genial about John Wayne's off-screen politics.

In the late 1940s, Duke Wayne was one of the founders of the Motion Picture Alliance for the Preservation of American Ideals, a McCarthy-era anti-Communist group, and increasingly his former non-partisan all-Americanism began to be associated with the brand of vocal right-of-centre politics that in the 1960s was reflexively pro-Vietnam War. In the

Duke's case, those politics led to *The Green Berets*, a film about the Special Forces in Vietnam that was made in the heroic mode of his World War II pictures.

By the time *The Green Berets* came out in 1968, huge anti-war demonstrations were taking place all across the country, and much of the young movie-going public of the time dismissed the picture, which the Duke starred in and co-directed, as being out of touch and politically reactionary. Although over the years the movie made money, it barely broke even in its initial American theatrical run.

Of course, from the beginning of cinema, some movies have advanced the political and social agendas of their filmmakers, from the pro-Klan histrionics of *The Birth Of A Nation* right up to the violent pieties of *The Passion Of The Christ*, and such other recent movies-with-a-message as the anti-fast food *Super Size Me*, the pro-environmental-movement *The Day After Tomorrow* and the anti-President Bush summer sensation, *Fahrenheit 9/11*.

A recent book about the actor, *John Wayne: The Man Behind The Myth*, by British author Michael Munn, makes the controversial allegation that the Duke's high-profile anti-Communism in those years came to the baleful attention of both Mao Zedung and Joseph Stalin, and that both Communist leaders tried on more than one occasion to have the Duke assassinated.

Munn is a former publicist, who met Wayne in 1974 when the actor was in London filming *Brannigan*, a minor policier. In the book, Munn tells of hearing a rumour the year before from actor Peter Cushing to the effect that Stalin had ordered the killing of a 'famous American cowboy star' in Hollywood. In his long career, Cushing played both 'Sherlock Holmes' and 'Dr Who', but is probably best known for appearing in a host of horror and monster movies, mostly in the 1950s and '60s. In London, Munn says, the Duke confirmed that the rumour was true and that he was that cowboy star.

With the help of the FBI, according to Munn, Wayne himself actually captured two of the would-be Commie killers Stalin dispatched, nabbing them at gunpoint in a movie studio in the early '50s. More than a decade later, Wayne also survived a sniper's attempt to shoot him when he was visiting the troops in Vietnam; that sniper presumably had been acting on Mao's orders.

True or not – and there are sceptics aplenty, who point out that there is no corroboration for the stories – the tales of would-be assassins foiled by Duke Wayne himself are utterly in keeping with the actor's larger-than-life heroic image.

And while the assassination story may sound like something out of, well, a B-movie, consider this: among those little boys all around the world growing up entranced by the American Dream they saw up on the silver screen was one who was born Iosif Vissarionovich Dzhugashvili, in the Republic of Georgia, but adopted the pseudonym 'Josef Stalin' when he grew up to become the dictator of the Soviet Union. Interestingly enough, 'Stalin' means a 'man of steel'.

Stalin, a prodigious drinker, loved watching Hollywood movies in his private screening rooms, and he particularly loved American Westerns. John Wayne was his favourite – at least until he learned that Wayne was a staunch, and influential, anti-Communist.

After one drunken screening, Stalin declared that Wayne was a menace to the Soviet cause and should be done away with, according to Simon Sebag Montefiore, author of *Stalin: The Court Of The Red Tsar*, writing in *The Telegraph*. The next morning, Stalin may have completely forgotten his drunken tirade, but his minions – as minions are wont to do – took him seriously, or so the argument goes.

In 1969, John Wayne won the Best Actor Oscar for his role in *True Grit*, playing 'Rooster' Cogburn, a tough, old, one-eyed Western marshal. The award, said his critics, was more for his persona than for his acting ability.

If so, as his fans around the world, who still regard him as the personification of the ideal American, will attest, it was still deserved.

Actors like Humphrey Bogart, James Cagney, Edward G Robinson and George Raft became famous in the gangster movies of the '30s and the noirs of the '40s, often playing Americans who were equally as compelling as hard-boiled tough guys and even out-and-out bad guys. Examples abound:

Bogart as private detective 'Sam Spade' in *The Maltese Falcon*, handing over the femme fatale who killed his partner to the police, saying – in a line of dialogue that practically defines hard-boiled: 'All we've got is that maybe you love me and maybe I love you... Maybe I do. I'll have some rotten nights after I've sent you over, but that'll pass.' Cagney as ' "Cody" Jarrett', the mad-dog killer with an Oedipus complex, in *White Heat*, shouting out, as a huge refinery tank blows up under him, 'Made it, Ma! Top of the world!' And Robinson as gang lord 'Cesare Enrico "Rico" Bandello' in *Little Caesar*, the influential 1930 mob epic, dying as violently as he lived, gasping out those famous last words of utter disbelief after he's been gunned down, 'Mother of Mercy! Is this the end of Rico?'

The character of Little Caesar was based on real-life gangster Alphonse 'Al' Capone, nicknamed 'Scarface' for the mark left on his cheek by a teenage knife fight. Capone was the Prohibition-era bootlegger who became Chicago's crime czar in the Roaring Twenties, when rival gangs fought for control of the illegal liquor, or 'bootlegging', business.

Capone, who rose to the top in these machine-gun street wars, is widely credited with creating the modern mob, along with his old mob buddy in New York, Charles 'Lucky' Luciano, born Salvatore Lucania. They, and their on-screen doppelgangers, have become emblematic of another, darker kind of American entrepreneur – the cutthroat, lawless empire builder, who used bullets to eliminate his enemies and racket money to infiltrate legitimate businesses and extend the mob's criminal reach into American society.

Today, organised crime is big, multinational business, but it wasn't always so big or so organised. Its roots go back to the great 19th-century waves of immigration into the United States, when La Cosa Nostra and the other bandit gangs that had oppressed the American newcomers in the Old Country began to prey on them in the New as well.

But ethnic gangs in the New World predate even the arrival of the Mafia. Of course, you can turn to Hollywood to learn all about it. *Gangs Of New York*, directed by Martin Scorsese, is a remarkably accurate (and violent) depiction of those early gang wars, during the mid-19th-century reign of Tammany Hall and Boss Tweed, when Irish immigrants banded together to battle 'nativist' gangs in the Five Points area of Old New York.

The impoverished immigrants who fled the Irish Potato Famine of 1846–50, which killed as many as one million people, often settled in the Five Points slum area of the Lower East Side, where they formed gangs like 'The Dead Rabbits', 'The Pug Uglies' and 'The Bowery Boys'.

By the end of the century, the Five Points was seething with Jewish, Italian and Irish gangsters, many of whom banded together in the Five Points Gang, under the charismatic leadership of Paul Kelly (who was born Paulo Antonini Vaccarelli), a dapper, multi-lingual one-time boxer, who was in many ways the model for later generations of Hollywood-influenced mobsters. In fact, in the early years of the 20th century, when they were still young men learning their criminal trade, both Luciano and Capone were members of New York's Five Points Gang.

Today, with new waves of immigrants there are new mafias – the Russian, the Vietnamese and so forth – but the original New York and Chicago organised-crime gangs – made up primarily of Italian and Jewish criminals escaping the tenements in the only way they knew – with bullets and machine guns – derived generally from the criminal enterprises of La Cosa Nostra, the Sicilian bandit network that formed the basis of the Five Families in New York, the Outfit in Chicago and associated mobs in Kansas City, New Orleans and elsewhere. And each mob had its own godfather, and all the godfathers were linked, thanks to Luciano's criminal vision, in a national commission of crime.

But in the imaginations of people all around the world, one American city above all came to symbolise the dapper crooks and bold outlaws glamorised by Hollywood in picture after picture.

Chicago.

Capone took control of the 1,000-gangster-strong Chicago mob when he was still in his mid-'20s. He and other Chicago Gangster Era mobsters like John Dillinger, 'Baby Face' Nelson, George 'Machine Gun' Kelly and 'Pretty Boy' Floyd have been portrayed over and over in movies and television programmes that have played all around the world. And they have become an indelible part of America's myth and 'cowboy' image.

In fact, say the name 'Capone' and most likely the blazing machine guns of the infamous St Valentine's Day Massacre come to mind. On 14 February 1929, Capone's mobsters eliminated the last gang standing between him and total underworld rule in Chicago – the Irish mobsters of the 'Bugs' Moran Gang. To this day, that event, which has been the subject of movies and TV shows ranging from *The Untouchables* to *Some Like It Hot*, is central to the brawny image of the city of Chicago, which for a lawless period in the twenties and thirties Capone's gang terrorised.

A dark street, a pool of light. Stepping from the shadows, a hard man in a fedora and a boxy suit, hand stuffed in a pocket, grasping something menacing, then...

A shiny black sedan screaming around a rain-slicked corner, machine gun blazing from the back window.

These iconic images of all those gang wars for control of lucrative rackets and turf that raked the city in the '20s and '30s have been – thanks to Hollywood – memorialised, and glamorised, in imaginations around the world.

To this day, visitors arrive in Chicago, a big, handsome, broad-shouldered metropolis – not to see the imposing skyline, the shopping streets of the Loop, the lake-front beaches, the world-class museums or the river meandering right through the middle of downtown – but to visit the sites of those long-ago gang wars.

George Raft was one actor of the period who specialised in portraying suave criminals and mob lords. He brought to his roles the authority of a poor childhood, growing up among actual hoods and gangsters, in New York's Hell's Kitchen (an area now known as Clinton, a fashionably hip neighbourhood on Midtown Manhattan's West Side). He first came to public attention in the 1932 film *Scarface*, starring Paul Muni, the other universally known gangster picture of the early sound period about the violent rise and fall of an ambitious mobster, loosely modelled after Al 'Scarface' Capone.

From the beginnings of the hard-hitting crime movie in the early '30s, there was an affinity between the real mobsters, who liked being glamorised on screen, and the actors who portrayed them. In fact, from the earliest days of the crime pictures, the gangsters watched the movies the better to learn how to be glamorous outlaws, while the actors hobnobbed with the crooks for the he-man frisson and the authenticity.

Prohibition, enacted in 1919 to rid the United States of the scourge of alcohol, instead made the mob big, offering undreamt-of opportunities for small-time crooks and neighbourhood ethnic gangs. At the height of his mob influence, no less a figure than Lucky Luciano lived in splendour in a suite at the Waldorf Astoria on posh Park Avenue, on the East Side of Manhattan, with his suave and handsome associate, Benjamin 'Bugsy' Siegel, ensconced in a suite a few floors below. They could be found most nights in the most glamorous nightclubs in the city, in the company of the most beautiful women and the most famous stars of the era, including both Frank Sinatra and Raft, an old pal of Siegel's, Luciano's close criminal friend.

If the dapper, dangerous-looking Raft didn't become as famous as his peers, that was less an accident than a matter of his fallible career choices. He famously turned down the lead roles in *High Sierra*, *The Maltese Falcon*, *Casablanca* and *Double Indemnity*, some of the most famous pictures in all of Hollywood movie history.

The most famous noir characters in American movies – detective Philip Marlowe, in *The Big Sleep*, and detective Sam Spade, in *The Maltese Falcon*, were created by two of the finest early crime-genre American novelists, Raymond Chandler (Marlowe) and Dashiell Hammett (Spade). Both iconic detectives were portrayed most definitively on screen by Humphrey Bogart. Chandler was the great LA noir novelist and screenwriter of the thirties and forties, while Hammett, who also created *The Thin Man*, was the premiere chronicler of fictional crime up the coast, in San Francisco. Of course, there were the screenplays by Billy Wilder and others, and novelists from James M Cain to Jim Thompson, who created memorable noir characters and stories. But it is Chandler and Hammett in particular that we think of when we recall the tough noir private cop in a city where it's always night, determined to solve the crime no one else wants to see uncovered, or the principled loner everyman, caught up in a convoluted conspiracy, making his way through a corrupt shadowy world.

During roughly the same period that Bogart was being lauded for his acting in those movies, which created his indelible screen persona, Raft starred in, among others, *They Drive By Night*, *Background To Danger*, *Nob Hill* and *Johnny Angel*. Not a bad group of films, to be sure, but no *Casablanca* or *Maltese Falcon* among them.

Bugsy Siegel travelled West to Los Angeles in the mid-1930s, to look after the Luciano mob's union and other interests there, and for a time he lived in George Raft's house.

In many ways, Raft and Siegel, who'd hung out together in the Prohibition-era New York speakeasies as young men, were mirror images of each other. According to one account, in Los Angeles they shared the same woman, Virginia Hill, the beautiful young mob moll that Siegel was to make famous, though apparently the mobster never knew his girlfriend was sleeping with his pal the actor too.

The blue-eyed Siegel was a mobster 'so good-looking and so gabby that he thought of being in pictures, an actor,' according to film historian David Thomson, while Raft was an actor 'so stiff and uneasy that he traded on the rumor that he knew big, bad wolves' in the mob. In the late '30s and early '40s, they might turn up together in the most famous LA nightclubs, places like the Brown Derby and Ciro's, a succession of starlets on Siegel's arm. Siegel used the Hollywood extra's union, which he ran, to extort money from the studios, and he had interests in a racetrack just over the border and a gambling ship just outside the reach of the local law. Which man modelled his persona after the other was, during their lifetimes, a subject of some debate.

Through Raft, Siegel became friends with actors from Cary Grant to Jimmy Durante, and with movie moguls like Jack Warner. And in an oddly symmetrical turn, later in his career, Raft was the on-premises celebrity host and casino manager in the Salon Rojo at the Capri, one of the Mafia-run casino-hotels in Havana, Cuba. In return for his services, mobsters Lucky Luciano and Meyer Lansky (the Jewish gangster with a head for numbers, who was fictionalised as 'Hyman Roth' and played by Lee Strasberg, in *Godfather II*) gave the actor a 'piece' of the Capri, making him a part owner. Raft played his tough-guy movie image there to the hilt.

On New Year's Day in 1959, Fidel Castro's ragtag rebel army suddenly overthrew the government of Cuban President Fulgencio Batista, who fled the country. The Mafia's reign in Havana had come to an abrupt and unexpected end. That night, celebrating mobs looted the glittering casinos. But, according to one famous story, Raft himself stopped the would-be looters at the Capri, confronting the mob at the entrance with this supposed warning: 'No punks are busting up my casino!' Faced with this formidable on-screen icon in person, the looters simply melted away.

A decade and a half or more earlier, Raft's mobster friend Bugsy Siegel had a transforming vision in the desert. The exact date of his first visit to a sleepy, dusty little town of some 6,000 souls, baking in the middle of the Nevada desert, three hundred miles down the road from LA, is lost to history. There were already brothels there and a few ramshackle, so-called 'sawdust' gambling joints, when Bugsy first arrived.

The local solons, in their wisdom, had made gambling legal in the state in 1931, and they made betting on horse races legal a decade later. The rough men who patronised the sawdust joints in the little town of Las Vegas were locals – desert rats, cowboys, ranchers and the army of tough construction workers who had arrived to build the nearby Hoover Dam in the mid-'30s and then stayed on.

Others have claimed part of the credit for Siegel's vision, including the founder of *The Hollywood Reporter*, one of Tinseltown's two daily showbusiness trade papers, but in a big-budget movie Hollywood itself ratified the consensus account: Bugsy Siegel, dapper gangster and gangland visionary, could see the future in that little desert outpost, just a few hours away by car from Los Angeles. He knew that the end of World War II would mean boom times for the American West, that air-conditioning was coming, that cheap air travel was coming and that a national network of highways was coming.

He believed that a first-class, air-conditioned pleasure palace, offering first-class Hollywood entertainment and utterly legal gambling and sports betting, rising in the middle of the desert, would attract would-be high rollers from all around the country. And he convinced Meyer Lansky, the mob's number-one money man, to invest.

The Flamingo, named in tribute to long-legged Virginia Hill and her nickname, wasn't the first casino built right on the highway leading from LA, on what would later become famous all around the world as the Vegas Strip, but it was by far the most opulent, not even remotely comparable to a mere sawdust joint. It opened, in a disastrous rush to completion, at the end of December 1946.

George Raft and a handful of celebrities were in attendance, and Jimmy Durante was the first act in the hotel's main room. But the hotel had opened before it was ready, and there was even an unusual and fierce desert rain storm on its opening night that kept most of the expected LA celebrities and high rollers away. The Flamingo's opening night, expected to be a glittering triumph, was instead a legendary disaster. And that was not lost on the hard-eyed mob financiers back East.

In its first weeks of operation, the Flamingo's casino even lost money, and for a time Siegel had to close its doors while construction continued. But after a few months, the Flamingo reopened and the money started to pour in. Meanwhile, Siegel's mob partners had become convinced that he had been cheating them, not only skimming profits from the casino but dollars from the construction over-runs, too. And the same month of the Flamingo's disastrous, stormy opening night in Vegas they secretly met in Havana and agreed that Benjamin 'Bugsy' Siegel had to go.

On the night of 20 June 1947, Siegel was staying at Hill's house in Beverly Hills. It was the end of a long day during which he'd spent time with his actor friend Raft. Bugsy Siegel sat down on the living room couch, facing the darkness on the other side of a picture window. That's where he was gunned down, killed in a hail of bullets from outside. Just minutes later, in distant Las Vegas, the Flamingo's new mob-installed bosses arrived to take over.

The story of modern Las Vegas's Founding Mob Father was a natural for Hollywood. A 1989 TV movie, *The Neon Empire*, co-written by New York newspaper columnist Pete Hamill, fictionalised the story. In *Bugsy*, a 1992 film directed by Oscar winner Barry Levinson, Bugsy Siegel was played by Warren Beatty, whose greatest success as an actor had come in *Bonnie And Clyde*, portraying another dangerous and boyishly charismatic real-life criminal. Long-legged Virginia Hill was played by Beatty's real-life wife, Annette Bening, whose own greatest earlier success was as a charming con artist in *The Grifters*, a latter-day film noir based on a novel by Jim Thompson.

By the late 1950s, Bugsy Siegel's mirage in the desert had become a mob-controlled neon oasis, with bundles of cash secretly skimmed from the casinos and sent back to the godfathers in Chicago, New York, Kansas City and elsewhere. In addition to the Flamingo, there was the Riviera, the Tropicana, the Desert Inn, the Fremont, the Landmark and others.

In the early '60s, no less an entertainer than Frank Sinatra was banned from owning a piece of a Nevada casino (in his case, the Cal-Neva in Reno) because of his associations with a known mobster, the Chicago Outfit's Sam Giancana (whose girlfriend, Judith Campbell, for a time was also the mistress of John F Kennedy, the glamorous young President of the United States).

In the late '60s, *Life* magazine published an influential exposé of the mob's infiltration of Las Vegas. And while that infiltration was widely known in high-roller and showbusiness circles, even adding to the desert town's cachet, other 'average' Americans were presumed to be shocked and reluctant to spend their holiday money in mobster-run establishments.

Enter Howard Hughes.

Hughes was a tough-as-hardwood American tycoon. As a teenager he'd inherited his father's company, Hughes Tool, which made drill bits for oil wells, and parlayed it to become one of the world's richest men, making his own fortune in oil and airlines. Early on, he was a producer of the original *Scarface* and the original *The Front Page*, and he directed *Hell's Angels*, a well-regarded early epic about dashing World War I fly boys in the Royal Air Force. He romanced beautiful movie stars, produced several of his own movies, owned his own Hollywood movie studio and flew (and sometimes crashed) experimental planes that he designed himself. In the '30s, he was at the controls of airplanes that set speed and distance records. In the '70s, he spied for the CIA, building a special salvage ship, the Glomar Explorer, to secretly raise a sunken Soviet nuclear submarine.

He was a tinkerer and an inventor, who created the first cantilevered push-up bra in the '40s, made especially for 19-year-old Jane Russell, when she starred in *The Outlaw*, the controversial and idiosyncratic movie he directed about Billy the Kid.

When he moved to Las Vegas in 1966, he bought a local television station, reputedly just so he could watch his favourite movies late at night. And if he fell asleep and missed a scene, he would phone a station engineer, have the film stopped and the scene replayed.

Hughes' exploits and his appetites were legendary, even before he became a germ-phobic, painkiller-addicted recluse in his last years. If his life sounds like the stuff of fiction and the movies, it is. In *The Carpetbaggers*, the Harold Robbins bestseller of some years back, he was fictionalised as *Jonas Cord*. And in *The Aviator*, a big-budget, big-screen film biography, directed by Martin Scorsese and scheduled for a Christmas 2004 release, he is played by Leonardo DiCaprio, with Cate Blanchett playing Katharine Hepburn, Kate Beckinsale playing Ava Gardner and rocker Gwen Stefani playing Jean Harlow.

Like Bugsy Siegel, in whose former suite at the Flamingo he lived, Howard Hughes understood Vegas and its potential, and he had scores of millions of dollars in cash at his ready disposal from his sale of Trans World Airlines.

Hughes – at a stroke – bought all the mob-controlled Vegas casino-hotels. In the aftermath of the *Life* magazine exposé, the casino-going public was presumed to be mollified. But in the counting rooms far from public view, mobsters were still skimming the profits.

In the mid-1970s, Hughes died and public control of the casinos shifted again. With the help of loans from the Teamsters Union, with which the mob had an association, a young businessman, whose company was called the Argent Corporation, bought out the casino interests of the Hughes Corporation. But Argent was fronting for old-line mobsters in Chicago and Kansas City, and soon the mob's men were back as casino bosses and key employees at casinos all up and down the Strip.

Of course, this period, when Wise Guys ruled the Strip, eventually was immortalised by Hollywood, in Martin Scorsese's epic *Casino*, starring Robert De Niro, Sharon Stone and Joe Pesci. That movie recounted, in fictionalised form, a famous actual mob love triangle of the early 1980s. The real players were Frank 'Lefty' Rosenthal, the mob-connected casino boss at the Stardust, Tony 'The Ant' Spilotro, the vicious mob hit man who was Lefty's childhood friend, and Geri, Lefty's beautiful and sexy young wife, who secretly was also having an affair with Tony 'The Ant'.

Once the mob was again ensconced in Vegas, mobsters forced the designated Argent Corporation front man, real-estate entrepreneur Allen Glick, to sell, allegedly because he'd begun interfering with the mob's man, Lefty. According to his later court testimony, Glick was called to a meeting with Lefty and Carl DeLuna, an 'underboss' in the Kansas City mob, in the office of a prominent local defence attorney, Oscar Goodman. There he was ordered to sell his interests in the company that owned the Vegas casinos.

The Kansas City underboss was 'vulgar and animalistic', Glick later testified. 'He stated that he and his partners were finally sick of having to deal with me and having me around and I could no longer be tolerated.'

Consulting a piece of paper in his hand, the underboss read off the name and age of each of Glick's children, Glick testified. If he didn't sell, the mobster told Glick, then 'one by one he'd have each one of my sons murdered'.

Glick sold immediately.

The story of the Argent Corporation casinos and the mob skim became public in a series of sensational mid-'80s trials of mob bosses from Kansas City and Chicago. Vegas attorney Goodman represented one of the heads of the Kansas City mob in one trial, in which the chief government witness against him was the man who formerly had been in charge of the skim at the Tropicana. In his opening remarks, defence attorney Goodman was scathing about the cooperating witness, now living under government protection, calling him a 'turncoat who lived his life as a lie'.

Attorney Goodman's client eventually pleaded guilty. The mid-'80s trials of the Chicago and Kansas City mob bosses ended with long prison terms for the top Chicago bosses, while the top Kansas City boss died of cancer before the start of the trial.

In the '90s, public corporations took over Las Vegas, cleaning up its unsavoury image and even imploding the old mob-run pleasure palaces and building huge new hotel-casinos that dwarfed anything ever seen on the Strip.

Today, King Arthur's Castle, Caesar's Palace, the New York Skyline and the Great Pyramid all coexist on the same broad, neon-lighted avenue, where there are no clocks and the action never stops. For a decade and more, Las Vegas billed itself as a family-friendly vacation destination and tourists poured in from all over the world.

And what of the '80s mob love triangle that was immortalised in *Casino*? Lefty (De Niro in the movie) survived a bomb blast that blew up his Cadillac. Asked who he thought was responsible for the bomb, Lefty replied, 'It wasn't the Boy Scouts of America.' Shortly thereafter, prudently, he left town. His wife (Sharon Stone in the movie) died of a drug overdose. Tony 'The Ant' (Joe Pesci in the movie) was brutally murdered, his body discovered by a farmer in an Indiana field.

In 1999, attorney Oscar Goodman, the colourful, self-described 'longtime lawyer for the mob', who had a bit part in *Casino* playing himself, and whose clients over the years also had included Meyer Lansky, was elected mayor of Las Vegas.

Early in the 21st century, Las Vegas gave up its long publicity campaign to erase any traces of its unsavoury past and to portray itself solely as a family-friendly tourist destination – a species of Disneyland for adults, but with lots of wholesome fun for the kids, too – and went back to trumpeting its original deliciously scandalous image, an image that people all around the world loved, just as they loved Chicago's old-time gangland associations.

Once again, Las Vegas was Sin City.

Of course, a nationwide TV commercial campaign was launched by the city's fathers. In January 2003, the Las Vegas Convention and Visitors Authority began to spend some $58 million on a 20-month-long television campaign. In one of those TV ads, a sexed-up young woman in the back of limousine is seen nuzzling the driver's ear during a nighttime ride from a casino out to the airport. But by the time the limo parks kerbside, the driver opens her door and she strides out, the young hottie in the backseat has morphed back into a bespectacled no-nonsense businesswoman, mobile phone to her ear, snapping out instructions to underlings. The commercial's ever-so-naughty tag line says it all...

What Happens Here Stays Here.

Why do Russian mobsters model themselves after American gangsters from the Roaring Twenties? Why do people all around the world love American crime stories, from *Scarface* to *The Sopranos*?

Shakespeare knew the answer. Villains, who dissembled and acted boldly, in their own utter self-interest and in defiance of society's rules, tended to overshadow heroes, who, after all, didn't have to be John Wayne to feel bound by a code. 'O villain, villain, smiling, damned villain!' brooded Hamlet. 'That one may smile, and smile, and be a villain!'

Villains had fun, too – Hollywood knew that – even if, traditionally, they were expected to pay for it in the final scene. In movies, screenplay writer Herbert Mankiewicz, who went on to write *Citizen Kane*, opined to young Ben Hecht upon his arrival in Hollywood, the villain 'can lay anybody he wants, have as much fun as he wants cheating and stealing, getting rich and whipping the servants. But you have to shoot him in the end.'

Hecht went on to write the screenplay for *Scarface*, and the stage plays on which *The Front Page* and *His Girl Friday* were based, as well as *Twentieth Century*, regarded by many as the definitive '30s screwball comedy.

Somewhere between the good guys and the bad guys are just the guys, but not all of them are content to struggle quietly and anonymously through an endless round of workdays, merely to put food on the table and to make ends meet.

America was founded by rebels and loners, hungry for the new frontier. 'We must indeed all hang together, or, most assuredly, we shall all hang separately,' Benjamin Franklin famously said on the very day in 1776 that the Declaration of Independence was signed. And whatever else it was, the remark was also a recognition that the founders were strong-willed individualists, who had to work together if they were to survive, much less succeed.

The country's governing myth is of loners pushing forward, beyond the horizon of the known, to the next frontier. That's been true from the days of Lewis and Clark right through to the astronauts and the ageing Boomers tooling around country highways on their Harleys. And the peoples of the world, for all the years of the country's existence, have flocked to the American frontier to take their part in the often perilous journey.

Is it any wonder that those American loners sometimes made their own laws? Or that popular culture – from the dime novel to the Hollywood blockbuster – romanticised them?

So such characters are found throughout American history, both real and mythic – from Davy Crockett at the Alamo to 'Sonny' Crockett in *Miami Vice*, from Buffalo Bill the Army scout to Buffalo Bill the showman, from Scarface the Chicago mob boss to *Scarface* the movie.

All those Hollywood heroes roaring by on motorcycles... Brando. McQueen. Cruise...

The Wild One. The Great Escape. Mission: Impossible 2.

In each of those emblematic, all-American action sagas, the motorcycle of choice turned out to be a British Triumph. In America, nobody was really upset that those big-screen bikes weren't all-American Harley-Davidsons at all. And that, boys and girls, is certainly another reason why people love the United States.

9 The Fresh New Thing: What's Next

Out there in the middle of the American desert improbable Las Vegas just keeps growing, the pulsing centre of one of the fastest growing counties in the United States. These days, there's even talk of building a high-speed rail line to connect Sin City with LA. Bigger, more lavish casino-hotels keep going up, and the slots keep getting more seductive too. You can safely bet that people from all around the world, fascinated by anything-goes Las Vegas or, like J Lo's mum, just hoping for their own big score, will keep arriving.

In Hollywood, they'll keep making TV shows and movies, sending them out to fascinated audiences not just in America but all around the world. Silicon Valley will keep making new high-tech gadgets and new applications for old ones; the revenues from its video-game businesses already exceed the box office total for all of Hollywood's movies. And soon, all that ephemeral Hollywood 'product'– no matter what the original medium – will be digitised and will be going out on the Internet; in fact, that's already well underway.

Only broadband penetration and piracy concerns stand between Hollywood and the pay-per-view premiere – on your very own state-of-the-art high-definition flat-screen surround-sound home-entertainment system – of a summertime theatrical-movie special-effects blockbuster. Everyone in Hollywood knows the right movie will take in $100 million or more – Ka-ching! – in a single night.

Even now some kid somewhere is surfing the Web, figuring out exactly how to do it so the studios, wary of online pirates, buy in. It doesn't matter anymore where this kid is, she could be munching a Big Mac, sipping a Starbucks or a Coke, sitting in front of a laptop in the Silicon Valley, in Singapore or Bangalore. Of course, she's dreaming of Hollywood or Vegas or New York, and of Making It Big, dreaming the very latest iteration of the American Dream.

The narratives of American popular culture have swept around the world, and one result is that distinctly American archetypes, American ambitions and American ideals are interwoven in the stories people everywhere tell themselves.

American movies, TV shows and music, even fast food and clothes – they all tell those stories all around the world. You can now add American magazines to the list of pop-culture artifacts that have gone global. *Cosmopolitan*, one of the bibles of fashionability, publishes fifty editions outside the United States, including *Cosmo Kazakhstan*. In all, Hearst, *Cosmo*'s publisher, publishes 135 international titles, from O the *Oprah* magazine to *Popular Mechanics*, in 28 languages, available in 100 countries outside the United States. The reason for the worldwide expansion is simple, according to an analysis in *The New York Times*, which also owns the *International Herald Tribune* (and is itself expanding internationally; for example, making agreements with France's *Le Monde* and Britain's *Daily Telegraph* to include inside those papers its own weekly branded news supplements): Global brands catering to globalised customers, particularly in eastern Europe and Asia, need global advertising vehicles, and Western (that is, US) magazines have a cachet for those newly globalised consumers that local publications can't match.

Of course, the publishing traffic is not entirely one way. The biggest successes in American publishing in recent years have been the transplanted British 'lad' magazines. And the hottest fad among hip, skateboarding American teens is Parkour, a French import by way of London, according to *The Times*.

Parkour blends the daredevil, flying-off-sloping-walls acrobatics of skateboarders with martial-arts and gymnastic moves, but dispenses entirely with the skateboards. The result: limber teenage kids in trainers, boys mostly, tearing off walls, leaping down stairs and jumping over railings, their natural exuberance and athleticism codified as a competition and turned into a game. And Parkour, called 'freerunning' in Britain, has spread wildly around the United States, its growth and cool quotient magnified of course by its appearance in TV advertisements and by the power of the Internet.

Young people are, generally speaking, the great engines of popular culture. They buy the jeans, listen to the music, go to the movies, live for the bling-bling and the Next Big Thing. Given that, something significant for the future of international popular culture is going to happen over the next two decades: despite the rapidly approaching Golden Years of the biggest single cohort in American history – the Baby Boomers, that is – the United States two decades from now will be a significantly younger country in relation to its major international competitors, particularly China and India. That Fountain of Youth effect is thanks partly to the expected effects of continuing immigration and partly to a higher per-capita birthrate in the US than in Europe, both eastern and western, and Japan.

Meanwhile, the populations of China and India will be ageing, partly because in both countries government policies have resulted in a rapidly declining fertility rate, with historically high levels of boys being born, rather than girls (partly as a result of the increased use of ultrasound to predict a foetus's sex, and partly because of old-fashioned local cultural attitudes that value girl babies less than boys). Coming years will see a 'bride deficit' in both of those huge countries, political economist Nicholas Eberstadt, a right-of-centre demographer and scholar associated with the American Enterprise Institute, predicted in an analysis of Asian-Pacific population trends.

In 2025, the United States will be the third most populous country in the world. But the US population then will be 'more youthful, and ageing more slowly, than that of China or any of today's [Asian economic] "tigers"', according to economist Eberstadt, who concluded that those demographic 'trends may, in some limited but tangible measure, contribute to the calculus of American strategic preeminence – in the Asia Pacific region, and indeed around the world'.

You can bet that in some 'limited but tangible measure' those same trends will 'contribute to the calculus' of American cultural vitality, and its continued preeminence there, too.

Americans truly believe they are the good guys of history, reluctantly riding to the rescue of those in peril; in the 20th century Americans acted on and died for that belief, and they continue to do so today.

America has always been a beacon. And despite the present obscuring gloom, despite the distortions and fears of wartime, it continues to be so today. If you doubt it, consider the message that the brave Chinese students were sending the world in the summer of 1989, when they gathered in Tiananmen Square in Beijing to demand freedom and democracy, and erected a 10m-(33ft)-tall statue they called the Goddess of Democracy. That styrofoam and papier mâché statue was a replica of the Statue of Liberty, which has greeted generations of immigrants in New York Harbor.

Forget for a moment high culture. Forget all those 19th-century starched-collar American millionaires out of Henry James novels buying up the glories of European civilisation, crating them up and shipping them back to mansions in the USA. Forget that the London Bridge of old nursery rhymes now sits in the Arizona desert, in Lake Havasu City. Think of the popular culture only. There you will find the adaptive American genius too. Whether the vaquero, the griot or reality television, America has always adopted the world's best. It's nothing new. Even the Wild West of reality was multicultural, with far-off, lawless outposts in the territories, places like Deadwood (now immortalised in HBO's gritty series *Deadwood*), actually aswirl with the ambitions of Chinese immigrants, Scandinavian settlers and Jewish entrepreneurs.

And why not? Despite America's faults and historical misdeeds, is it not the Melting Pot, a mongrel – or if you prefer, a mustang – country, not like the high-falutin' lands of the Old Country? If you doubt America's vitalising variety, go to any airport in any big American city and marvel at the types passing through. As the song says, 'We Are The World'. Madison Avenue has gotten that message, and demography and the United States Census bear this insight out: the United States of America is getting browner, more Hispanic, more Asian. If 'demography is destiny', as the French mathematician said, then, soon, all of America will look like the multicultural National Basketball Association, only presumably not quite as tall.

Why do people love the United States? Basically, it's because of its unparalleled freedoms and opportunities, and that exuberant, not always well-behaved, pop culture. Plus Americans are cool, they're bad-asses and good guys, too. Nature's Noblemen, you might say.

Why do people from all around the world keep travelling to America? Whoever they are, wherever they're from, they can look and find themselves there. It turns out that what people love about America is what they love about themselves.

Gentle Readers, this book has been big fun to write, and I trust it partially pays an ancient debt I've owed to Uncle Sam ever since arriving on America's shores.

'I know no safe depository of the ultimate powers of the society but the people themselves,' America's second president once wrote. I take heart from that.

It's a big country, and there are a great many reasons to love it, just as there are an inexhaustible number of American dreams. In fact, it's far too big and there are far too many reasons to squeeze into one small book. And I know that, among many others, a certain internationally famous cartoon mouse has been slighted in these pages, as well as the entire city of Memphis, Tennessee, home of Sun Studio, where in 1954 Elvis recorded his first record. Perhaps I'll have the opportunity to make it up to Mickey and the King in a second edition. So, if you'd like to make suggestions for other things to include in future iterations of this book, or if you'd just like to comment on the present one, here's how to do it: email me at <u>Lchunovic@aol.com.</u>

Citations

Introduction: Greetings From The Capital Of The World

Guadalupe hits the jackpot – The *Guardian*, 7 April 2004

'Wet foot, dry foot' – *St Petersburg Times*, 10 October 2003

Oprah doubts – TV executive Dennis Swanson in a conversation with the author

Calling Castro – *LaMusica*, 18 June 2003

Paying the fine with pennies for calling Castro – *Radio and Records*, 30 April 2004

The Apprentice finale – Associated Press, 16 April 2004

Richards discovers that Jagger, too, loves the Chicago blues – *Playboy*, April 1995

The death of Pat Tillman – Associated Press, 23 April 2004

President Clinton quote – *Hartford Courant*, 3 December 2001

Madrassahs and dinosaurs – *ibid*

Gays out on a limb – *New York Daily News*, 23 April 2004

Princess Michael of Kent allegedly rebukes a group of African-American diners – *New York Post*, 26 May 2004, and *The New York Times*, 28 May 2004

Mad Ave Sells America (And The Rest Of The World Eagerly Buys)

Charlotte Beers's remarks – transcript from *The Newshour With Jim Lehrer*, on PBS, January 2003

US propaganda film produced before the first Gulf War, Rough quote – January 2004, *Heritage Lecture Series*, No.187

The Marketplace Of Revolution reviewed – *New Yorker*, 16–23 February 2004

President of the Heritage Foundation's remark about Ben Franklin – *ibid*

East Germans want oranges and music – *Fortune*, 31 December 1990

David Hasselhoff sings at the Berlin Wall – BBC News, February 2004

'And, in due course, apartheid fell' – a sentiment expressed in a conversation the author had with Brandon Tartikoff, the late NBC television programming executive responsible for putting *The Cosby Show* on the air

Professor Potter quote – *Collier's Encyclopedia*, Vol.I, p136, 1992

Coke as a South African brand – *Sunday Times* of South Africa, October 2003

Coke as best brand in the UK – PR Newswire, 8 October 2003

Leo Burnett quote – *Fortune*, 10 May 1999

Madison Avenue in India – *Business Today*, 20 January 2002

Joe Uva's travels – from a conversation with the author

Ike Herbert's slogans and jingles for Coke – American Advertising, spring 1995

Timex, the most recognisable brand – *Women's Wear Daily*, 24 January 2000

Coke follows the troops in World War II – *Fortune*, 10 May 1999

McDonald's statistics – *Sunday Business*, 27 February 2000

Super Size Me as 'effective agitprop' – *Philadelphia City Paper*, 8–14 April 2004

Peter Rainer review – *New York* magazine, 10 May 2004

Ray Kroc, brand zealot – *Fortune*, 10 May 1999

Big Mac and Tall Latte Indices – Wikipedia.org, an online encyclopedia

Dubai McDonald's franchisee on the McArabia sandwich – *The New York Times*, 15 March 2003

McDonald's in the Middle East – statistics available at the company's website

Americanisation of Egyptian pop culture – *Al-Ahram*, 26 February and 3 March 2004

Painting Manhattan manhole covers with the Pepsi logo – Mediacom executive Jon Mandel; from a conversation with the author

Finalists for the Advertising Walk of Fame – *Adweek*, 26 April 2004

Warrant Officer Hugh Thompson, Junior, stops the My Lai Massacre – Wikipedia.org

Michael Caine loves America – *New York Post*, 28 April 2004

'War and Abuse Do Little Harm to US Brands' – *The New York Times*, 9 May 2004

Survey of international consumers' views of America finds downtrend – *Advertising Age*, 6 May 2004

Countries with least and most affinity for American culture, according to a survey – *ibid*

Elinor Burkett in Central Asia and elsewhere finds both anti-Americanism and a longing for American help – *Chronicle of Higher Education*, 23 April 2004

American movies in Iraq, *The New York Times*, 13 April 2004

Hollywood And The Great American Myth Machine (Optioning Britain's Best)

Mid-'80s positive trade balance of $1 billion – *Canadian Journal Of Communication*, Vol.19, No.3/4, 1994

Statistics: more than half of theatrical film revenues are from outside the US – *Business & Management Practices*, Vol.44, No.6, 2001

Japanese marketing consultant quote – *Fortune*, 31 December 1990

The media business is called *omizu shobai*, or the 'water business', in Japan – *ibid*

Frederic Raphael quote – *The New York Times*, 6 January 1985

Cecil B DeMille gives Flagstaff a pass – *Tucson Weekly*, 19 and 25 April 2001

Arnold Schwarzenegger's estimated net worth and his real-estate holdings – *Los Angeles Business Journal*, 11 August 2003

Arnold Schwarzenegger disavows political ambitions – conversation with the author during the press junket for *Terminator 2: Judgment Day*

Statistics: French and Canadian quotas – *Business & Management Practices*, op. cit.

German film quotas in the 1920s – *International Journal Of The Economics Of Business*, Vol.7, No.1, February 2000

Former Canadian Prime Minister Kim Campbell quote – globalisation.org, a website of the Center For Strategic & International Studies

Five hundred billion dollars in annual sales for entertainment and intellectual property – *Los Angeles Daily News*, 14 March 2003

MPAA ShoWest production and marketing data – *Variety*, 29 March 2004

MPAA's Jack Valenti on the human condition – United Press International, 9 October 2002

'The Big B' is the star of the millennium – *Newsweek International*, 28 February 2000

Bollywood's 2002 box-office disaster – *Asia Pacific Arts* (a publication of the UCLA Asia Institute), no date available

Bollywood's science-fiction hit – *Asia Pacific Arts*, 9 April 2004

Bollywood on Broadway – *The New York Times*, 26 April 2004

Business For Diplomatic Action formed to combat a declining 'regard' for all things American – *Advertising Age*, 11 May 2004

Seattle: Microsoft And Starbucks – Code And Coffee Conquer The World

Starbucks's corporate timeline – official company history

Philosophy and 'mystery and romance' of coffee – *Pour Your Heart Into It: How Starbucks Built A Company One Cup At A Time*, by Howard Schultz and Dori Jones Yang, Hyperion, 1997

Bill Gates Senior was Howard Schultz's lawyer – *Fortune*, 26 January 2004

Earliest version of Windows – Wikipedia.org

Legal jujitsu – *The New York Times*, 17 February 2003

Microsoft and Sun settle – *The New York Times*, 3 April 2004

Courtney Love embodies the grunge aesthetic and is a napalm feminist – *Women's Studies in Communication*, 22 September 2001

Kurt Cobain's mother's quote – *Newsweek*, 18 April 1994

'Smells Like Teen Spirit'– lyrics by Kurt Cobain

San Francisco: Sex, Drugs, The Rise Of Youth Culture (And Personal Liberation Movements)

The derivation of Brando's famous line in *The Wild One* – from *Stanley Kramer: Filmmaker*, by Donald Spoto; noted at TurnerClassicMovies.com

Mark Twain newspaper reports – *San Francisco Daily Morning Call*, July 1864

History of the Student Nonviolent Coordinating Committee's Mississippi Summer Project – from Encarta Africana

Free-form FM radio, the Monterey Pop Festival and the birth of *Rolling Stone* magazine – *Entertainment Weekly*, 28 May 1999

Women's liberation in the Bay Area – from *Shaping San Francisco*, a CD-ROM, and from an article by Professor Linda Gordon in the *Encyclopedia Britannica*

San Francisco population statistics – US Census Bureau

Disney buys Hewlett-Packard's first product – official H-P company history

H-P revenues – *ibid*

Professor Martin Kenney on the importance of Fairchild and its 'Fairchildren' – *Newsweek*, 30 April 2002

More than two dozen Fairchildren started by former Fairchild employees – *Business History Review*, Spring 2001

Semiconductor definition – Nanoelectronics.com

The Silicon Valley company creation myth – historian Paul Mackun, quoted in *Computer Weekly*, 30 November 2000

US Defense Department buys all the integrated circuits in the early 1960s – *Business History Review*, op. cit.

Santa Clara county employment rates, 1941–75 – *Business History Review*, op. cit.

A good contract is sealed with a line of coke – *Inc.*, July 1985

Al Ries quote – *Darwin* magazine, July 2001

Bill Nguyen is ready to party – *Forbes*, 8 December 2003

Venture capitalists invest in Google – *The New York Times*, 2 May 2003

Google's ping-pong table – official company history

Google's founders talk about 'building space transporters and implanting chips in people's heads' – *The New York Times*, 25 April 2004

Google's corporate culture in the early days – company history

Seventh Avenue: How The Rag Trade Became Haute Couture

History of Levi's – *The New York Times*, 4 October 1999

Definition of 'denim' – *Daily News Record*, 31 December 2001

List of premium jeans makers – *The New York Times*, 27 April

Pauline Trigere quotes – *Women's Wear Daily*, 15 February 2002

John Fairchild on Jackie Kennedy – *Women's Wear Daily*, 16 July 2001

Vivien Westwood's shops and contributions – *The New York Times*, 21 April 2004

Charles Kumar's story – *Inc.*, November 1984

Abe Schrader's story – *Smithsonian*, August 1985

Ralph Lauren and Calvin Klein biographies – Fashion Industry Information Services (infomat)

Versailles fashion showdown – *Women's Wear Daily*, 28 May 2002 and 5 August 2003

Renzo Rosso quote – *Daily News Record*, 15 September 2003

Diesel's 25th anniversary party – *ibid*

After Six history – *Daily News Record*, 10 February 2003

A history of super models – *Women's Wear Daily*, 16 July 2001

Eleanor Lambert creates Fashion Week – *Women's Wear Daily*, 6 August 2003

New York Fashion Week, 11 September 2001 – *Milwaukee Journal Sentinel*, 8 February 2002

London Fashion Week, 2001 – *The Guardian*, 17 September 2001

Senator Schumer quote and Senator Clinton's made-in-New York suit – *Women's Wear Daily*, 25 November 2002

Courtside At The Garden: The Thrill Of Victory, The Object Lesson Of Defeat

Knicks' ticket costs – Askmen.com

Howard Rubenstein quote – *Crain's New York Business*, 31 May 31 and 6 June 1993

Latrell Sprewell quote – *Newsday*, 26 March 2003

Players' quotes about New York street ball – *Sports Illustrated*,

NBA Commissioner's Disney quote – *Sports Illustrated*, 3 June 1991

Yao Ming biography – *Time For Kids*, 7 February 2003

Shaq discovered in Germany – *New Yorker*, 20 May 2002

'Miracle On 138th Street' – *New York Post*, 14 December 2003

Marilyn Monroe quote – *Ms* Magazine, August 1972

Alistair Cooke on Ali at the Garden – *The Guardian*, 7 March 2001

Michael Jordan gets the flag – *Jet*, 5 May 2003

Michael Jordan's $450 million in endorsement deals – *New Yorker*, 20 May 2002

Harlem: Home Of The First Black Ex-President And Now A Tourist Magnet For The World

Clinton quote – CNN, 31 July 2001

Clinton drops into Starbucks in Harlem – *USA Today*, 15 February 2004

Description of the rally welcoming Clinton to Harlem – *Jet*, 20 August 2001

Clinton's architect and P Diddy – United Press International, 19 April 2001

Harlem history, 1658–1904 – HometoHarlem.com

Pygmy in the zoo – *New Yorker*, 8 March 2004

'An expression of cultural nationalism' – *Black Renaissance/Renaissance Noire*, Summer 2002

Diaghilev's secretary's complaint about Cole Porter – *City Journal*, Winter 2003

'Saved' lyrics and significance – *Popular Music And Society*, 22 September 2001

Soul Cinema – *Brandweek*, 21 October 2002

Paul Winley on rap's sources from *Rap Attack 2* – *Playboy*, June 1996

Kool DJ Herc innovates the scratch – *ibid*

'Rapper's Delight' – lyrics by Sugar Hill Gang

'The Message' – lyrics by Grandmaster Flash

Roxy Tour plays for Her Majesty – *Philadelphia Inquirer*, 10 March 2004

'Sun City' on MTV – *Sunset*, 1 October 2001

Russell Simmons biography – *Business Week*, 27 October 2003

Kimora Lee Simmons bids on Blahniks – *New York Post*, 19 April 2004

Gil Scott-Heron arrested for cocaine possession – *Village Voice*, 18–24 July 2001

P Diddy biography – *Rolling Stone* online

Sean John Clothing's 2003 revenues – *The New York Times*, 13 May 2004

McWhorter quote – *City Journal*, Summer 2003

Nelly college protest – Associated Press, 23 April 2004

'Rhetoric of resistance' – *Western Journal Of Black Studies*, 22 December 2002

Harlem Club: ugly women need not apply – *The New York Times*, 21 April 2004

Damon Dash quote – *Business Week*, 27 October 2003

Alan Lomax collects royalties – *New Republic*, 16 June 2003

Chris Rock quote – *The New York Times*, 26 March 2004

Tim Duffy and the Music Maker Foundation – ABC News, 30 April 2004

More than 100 hip-hop millionaires – *Prospect*, March 2004

'The N-Word' documentary – Cynopsis.com, 27 April 2004

Car ads targeting African-Americans, *Brandweek*, 14 April 2003

Prince William's rap – *Prospect*, March 2004

From Purple Sage And Blazing Guns to Black-Top Highways And The Neon City: Good Guys, Bad Buys And The Rise Of Rebel Chic

The first cowboy was a vaquero – *National Geographic*, 15 August 2003

Mestizo vaqueros drove cattle for criollo landowners – *ibid*

Cowboy terms and practices deriving from the vaqueros – from Nps.gov

Timeline, 1821–48 – The Museum of Westward Expansion

The cowboy's uniform – from Nps.gov

Ned Buntline, prolific dime novelist, convinces Buffalo Bill to go into acting – *Columbia Electronic Encyclopedia*

Cowboy stars of the silent era – from the National Cowboy Museum

Tim McCoy biography – from the Internet Movie Database's mini-biography, by Jim Beaver

The Cowboy Code – from GeneAutry.com

Ronald Reagan about John Wayne – *Reader's Digest*, October 1979

John Wayne biography – from Jwplace.com

John Wayne survives Communist assassination attempts – recounted by author Michael Munn, BBC Radio, 30 July 2003

Virginia Hill slept with both George Raft and Bugsy Siegel – from *Bugsy's Baby: The Secret Life Of Mob Queen Virginia Hill*, by Andy Edmonds, Birch Lane Press, 1993

Bugsy Siegel and George Raft, described by David Thomson – *New Republic*, 22 August 1994

Siegel in Hollywood – *Playboy*, February 1992; an article by Pete Hamill, who also wrote *The Neon Empire*, a TV miniseries about Siegel

George Raft at the Capri in Havana – *US News & World Report*, 12 January 1998

George Raft faces down the Havana mob – *The Globe and Mail*, 10 March 2004

The death of Bugsy Siegel – *Playboy*, February 1992; op. cit.

Chronology of the history of the mob in Las Vegas – some of this material is taken from an unpublished manuscript, by the author, which in turn is based on several episodes of the television documentary series *American Justice*, hosted by Bill Kurtis, which airs in the United States on the Arts & Entertainment cable network

Glick told to sell or his children would be murdered – *The New York Times*, 9 November 1985

Oscar Goodman calls a government witness a 'turncoat' – *The New York Times*, 12 June 1983

Oscar Goodman's clients included Meyer Lansky – *The New York Times*, 26 January 2001

The cost and duration of the Las Vegas TV ad campaign – *Las Vegas Review-Journal*, 29 December 2003

The Triumph in three emblematic American films – *Fortune Small Business*, April 2002

The Fresh New Thing: What's Next

The New York Times goes international with new supplements – *New York Post*, 25 March 2004

American magazines go global as advertising vehicles for new global consumers – *The New York Times*, 13 February 2004

Parkour comes to the United States – *The New York Times*, 28 March 2004

Demographic trends in Asia and the US in 2025 – *Policy Review*, No.123; no date; adapted from *Strategic Asia, 2003–2004* (National Bureau of Asian Research), a study by Nicholas Eberstadt

Index